THE HISTORY OF
SINGAPORE

LION CITY, ASIAN TIGER

THE HISTORY OF
SINGAPORE

LION CITY, ASIAN TIGER

John Wiley & Sons (Asia) Pte Ltd

Other Wiley Editorial Offices

John Wiley & Sons, Inc., 111 River Street, Hoboken, NJ 07030, USA
John Wiley & Sons Ltd, The Atrium, Southern Gate, Chichester P019 8SQ, UK
John Wiley & Sons (Canada) Ltd, 5353 Dundas Street West, Suite 400, Toronto, Ontario, M9B 6HB,
        Canada
John Wiley & Sons Australia Ltd, 42 McDougall Street, Milton, Queensland 4064, Australia
Wiley-VCH, Boschstrasse 12, D-69469 Weinheim, Germany

Library of Congress Cataloging-in-Publication Data
978-0470-82320-0

Typeset in 11points, Rotis Serif by Hot Fusion
Printed in Singapore by Toppan Security Printing Pte. Ltd.
10 9 8 7 6 5 4 3 2 1

CONTENTS

RAFFLES' LITTLE CHILD

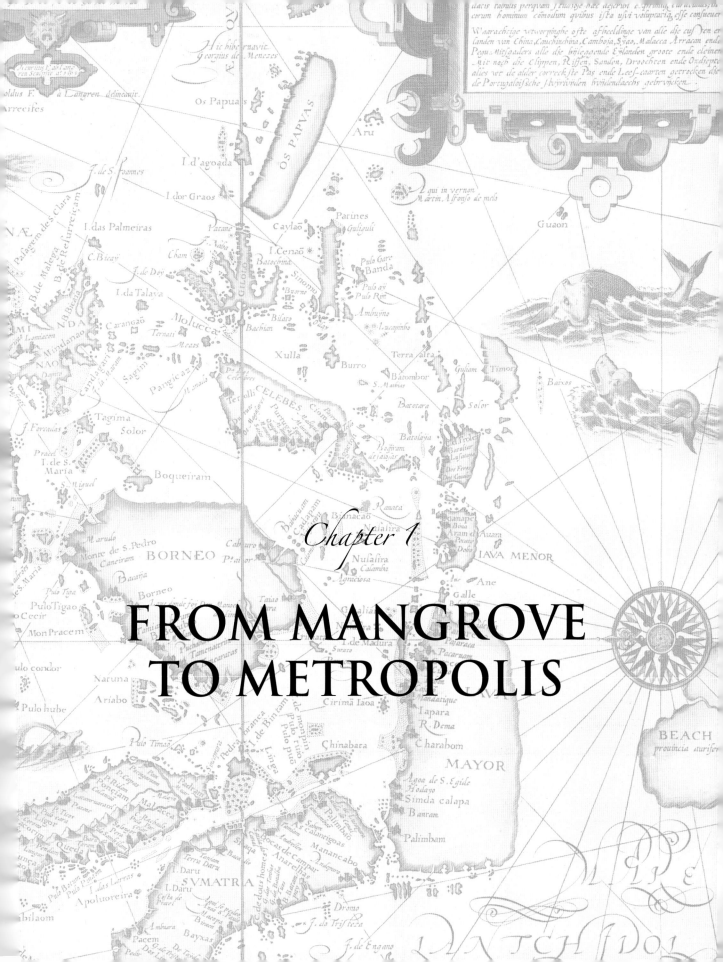

Chapter 1

FROM MANGROVE
TO METROPOLIS

4

When a small expeditionary force under the command of the British East India Company set out for the tiny island at the southern tip of the Malay Peninsula in January 1819, few could have imagined this trip would launch the development of a global economic powerhouse.

The island was just a bit of swamp separated from the peninsula by a narrow strait. It had no natural resources and was known chiefly as a base for Malay pirates who plied the local seas. A few fishing and farming villages dotted the island, but there was little else. Early Chinese maps of the region noted a village on the island called *Temasek*, "sea town" in Javanese. The island was also known by the Malay name *Singapura*, "lion city," after a legend that said a Malay prince visited the island in the 13th Century and was mistakenly told an animal he espied was a lion.

Those names would fade into history. The expedition by the East India Company led by a young and ambitious company officer named Thomas Stamford Raffles put "Singapore" on the map and set the stage for the island's improbable journey from an obscure backwater to a prosperous hub in the global economy.

When Raffles' ship, the *Indiana*, approached the island, Britain already possessed a powerful trading empire around globe, but was challenged in Southeast Asia by the Dutch. Raffles' exploratory team set out from the British enclave of

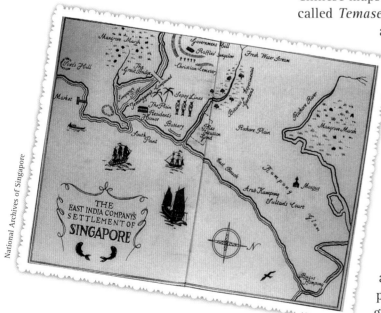

National Archives of Singapore

Map of the East India Company's settlement of Singapore, 1819. When Raffles arrived, the island was home to pirates, fishermen and farmers.

Preceding page: A late 16th century Dutch map of Southeast Asia, oriented with east at the top, showing "Singapura" at the center of the region.

Roger-Viollet/AFP

*Views of Singapore Roads
and river, circa 1860.*

Bencoolen, a pepper-trading and garrison town on the south-western coast of Sumatra, to help maintain and expand British influence in the area. He had studied early maps of the region and knew about Temasek, which had centuries earlier been the capital of a thriving Malay kingdom. While he eventually undertook an archaeological survey of the island, Raffles' focus was much more on the future than the past.

Raffles had come in search of a new settlement to replace Malacca, a major British trading centre that was to be passed to the Dutch as part of the peace settlement that ended the Napoleonic Wars. To replace Malacca, the new settlement would have to be a viable trading post, and, by extension, a base from which the British could defend their shipping lines from Dutch competition in the region.

The British had no legal claim to operate on the island. Singapura was part of the territory ruled by the Sultan of Johore, Tengku Abdul Rahman, though in reality the Sultan had very little authority there. The island

5

"Unless you know where you came from, unless you know what your ancestors have been through, you have no reference point. What makes us different from say the Thais or the Filipinos or the Sri Lankans? The difference is how we came here, how we developed and that requires a sense of history."

– Lee Kuan Yew, first prime minister of Singapore

6

Hulton Archive / Getty Images

1810 portrait of Sir Thomas Stamford Raffles, founder of the British colony of Singapore.

was governed by a headman, the Temenggong (also, as it happens, called Abdul Rahman). Sultan Abdul Rahman had ruled out any dealings with the British, but his elder brother, Hussein, had other ideas. Hussein felt cheated from the throne of the sultanate, and he saw that allying with the British would help him claim the throne. Raffles arranged for Hussein to be smuggled onto Singapura, where he promptly proclaimed Hussein the rightful sultan. "He (Raffles) was a man with vision, ahead of his time, perhaps," Julian Davidson, author of many books on Southeast Asia including "One for the Road," told Discovery Channel. "Whereas most of the East India Company officials were basically here for the trade, perhaps for the adventure, Raffles had an idea of changing the world, of making it a better place."

CHRONOLOGY OF SIR THOMAS STAMFORD RAFFLES' LIFE

1781	6 July	Raffles born at sea off Jamaica.
1795		Begins career at East India Company as a clerk at the age of 14.
1805	March	Appointed assistant-secretary to the governor of Penang, Philip Dundas.
	14 March	Marries Olivia Marianne Fancourt at St George's, Bloomsbury.
	September	Arrives in Penang.
1810	December	Moves to Malacca.
1811		Raffles prepares for the British invasion of Java.
	August	Fall of Batavia.
	September	Appointed lieutenant-governor of Java.
1814	November	Olivia dies.
1816	March	Succeeded by John Fendall as lieutenant-governor of Java.
	July	Arrives in England on leave. While there he writes "History of Java," which together with his other achievements, earn him a knighthood.
1817	February	Marries Sophia Hull at St Marylebone Parish Church, London.
	May	Receives knighthood from the prince regent.
	October	Raffles and Sophia sail for Bencoolen.
1819	January	Leads expedition from Bencoolen to island at tip of Malay Peninsula
	February	Signs treaty with Sultan Hussein and Temenggong Abdul Rahman establishing Singapore as a British colony.
1820–1824		Spends time in Bencoolen, Calcutta and Singapore.
1824	April	Leaves with Sophia for England.
1825	July	Takes up residence at Highwood.
1826	5 July	Dies at Highwood, one day before his 45th birthday. The cause of death is unconfirmed but is widely reported to be a brain tumour.

7

RAFFLES THE NATURALIST

During his time in the East Indies, Raffles developed a fascination for the massive diversity of flora and fauna, most of which were completely new to him. In one of his letters to a friend back in Britain, Raffles wrote, "I have a long list of animals, of which nothing yet is known beyond the name and native description." Raffles would pay his assistants out of his own pocket to collect specimens, which he then sent for analysis by zoologists and botanists. He became president of the Batavian Society, which, among other things, concerned itself with the study of the natural history of Java and the surrounding area.

Roger-Viollet/AFP

Singapore Botanic Gardens, circa 1900.

In her memoirs, Raffles' second wife, Sophia, wrote that his zoological collection included tapirs, rhinoceroses and deer, all of which were sent to Britain. Other animals in the collection, including a sun bear cub, were reared as pets in the Raffles home. Sophia reported that her husband was joined for dinner by creatures that sat down to eat mangoes and drink Champagne. "Two young tigers and a bear were for some time in the children's apartments, under the charge of their attendant, without being confined in cages, and it was rather a curious scene to see the children, the bear, the tigers, a blue mountain bird and a favourite cat, all playing together," Sophia wrote.

When Raffles sailed to Britain in 1824 a fire on board his ship, *Fame*, destroyed the huge collection of plant and animal specimens, notes and drawings that he had brought with him.

As Raffles was a celebrated contributor to the study of natural history, it is not surprising that a number of animals and plants have been named after him. Perhaps the most distinctive is the *Rafflesia*, a plant parasite that grows on palm trees. Raffles discovered and documented the plant on an expedition into the Sumatran jungle. The Rafflesia is endemic to Southeast Asia and produces the world's largest flower, which is also remarkably foul-smelling.

Getty Images

The Rafflesia produces the world's largest flower.

THE SHORT LIVES OF RAFFLES' CHILDREN

Raffles did not have any children with his first wife, Olivia Marianne. After Olivia died in 1814, Raffles married Sophia Hull. Together, they had five children but tragically, all but one died in infancy. Their first child, Charlotte, (1818-1822) was born at sea, as the family travelled from Britain to Bencoolen. Charlotte Raffles was said to be a gifted child and a linguist—by age three speaking English, Malay and Hindustani. In a letter home, Raffles described Charlotte as "the most angelic I ever beheld". He wrote that his daughter had "those inborn graces which, as she expands, must attract the admiration of everyone. But she has a soft heart, and is so full of mildness and gentleness, that I fear she will have many trials to go through in this unfeeling world."

Charlotte died at the age of four, just 10 days after the death of her younger brother, Stamford Marsden (1820-1822). Marsden was named after his godfather, the historian of Sumatra, William Marsden, and was nicknamed "Marco Polo" (in 1818 William Marsden had published an account of Marco Polo's travels). Raffles remarked that this child, like the others, had been blessed with "intelligence and disposition".

Leopold Stamford (1819-1821) likely died of cholera. Raffles described Leopold as "by far the finest child of all three; he is handsome, bold and intelligent, and struts about the house with an air of the most complete independence".

Sophia wrote of Leopold's death, "Upwards of three years had passed in uninterrupted health and happiness, but a sad reverse took place at this period; the blessings most prized were withdrawn; the child most dear to the father's heart, whose brightness and beauty were his pride and happiness, expired in all the bloom of infancy, after a few hours' illness; but God's Holy

Spirit enabled him to receive these afflictions with meekness, and to feel that they were trials of faith, not judgements of anger."

After the deaths of his children, Raffles decided to leave the region.

"We have this morning buried our beloved Charlotte. Poor Marsden was carried to the grave not ten days before, and within the last six months, we have lost our three eldest children: judge what must be our distress. This is a melancholy day, and I have turned my thoughts to serious subjects: among the rest, to the risk we run by remaining longer in this country. I have, therefore, taken the first steps towards going home, by sending in my resignation.

"We who had recently such a large and happy circle. All our fears were once that we should have too many: all our cares are now to preserve one—our only one. My heart is sick and nigh broken."

Ella Sophia (1821-1840) was the only child who survived childhood. She died in Britain at the age of 19, on the eve of her marriage. Their last child, Flora Nightingall (1823) survived a mere two months.

11

On 6 February 1819, a little more than a week after he anchored off Singapura, Raffles signed a treaty with Sultan Hussein and the Temenggong giving the British rule over the island. In exchange, the Sultan would receive 5,000 Spanish dollars annually and the Temenggong 3,000 Spanish dollars. (The Spanish dollar, also known as pieces of eight, was a silver coin that had gained currency throughout the world, particularly in North America and Southeast Asia.) At the conclusion of the signing, the Union Jack was raised over Singapore for the first time.

The historic ceremony at which authority over the island was ceded to the British was witnessed by just a handful of sailors, soldiers, pirates and fishermen, at the beginning of February 1819. Few could have understood the significance or the eventual impact of the event. Many of those who stood watching around the treaty table were seeing Europeans for the first time, and the meaning of the ceremony must have remained elusive.

12

Roger-Viollet/AFP

Raffles Institution was founded in 1823 by Stamford Raffles. It is the oldest school in modern Singapore and lists among alumni two prime ministers—Lee Kuan Yew and Goh Chok Tong.

Today skyscrapers attest the endurance of Raffles' vision of Singapore as a global economic center.

From a small Malay fishing village, the new Temasek would now be a British settlement in the hands of the East India Company. But what did that mean? How would life for the inhabitants change? What would life be like for the new settlers who would soon begin streaming into the island? How would Raffles turn a mangrove swamp into a city?

The British East India Company was at this time the largest corporation in the world. From its headquarters in London it directed the affairs of more than a fifth of the world's population, the bulk of its subjects on the continent of India, most of which was ruled by the company. It had its own civil service and its own army. The company's network of trade routes stretched across the globe, and in its heyday, its revenue was larger than that of Britain as a whole.

Not only did Raffles' vision of a bustling entrepôt in the heart of Southeast Asia endure, his name too was perpetuated in the settlement he established. Singapore abounds with places, institutions and public buildings named after its founder. Here are some of them:

THE RAFFLES NAME

CLUBS	Raffles Country Club Raffles Marina Raffles Town Club
SCHOOLS	Raffles Girls' School Raffles Institution Raffles Junior College
ROADS AND SQUARES	Raffles Avenue Raffles Boulevard Raffles Link Raffles Place Raffles Institution Lane

BUILDINGS /OTHER PLACES	Raffles Hotel (national monument)
	Raffles Hospital
	Raffles Place MRT Station
	Raffles Place (formerly Commercial Square)
	Raffles Place Park (park at Raffles Place)
	Raffles City
	Raffles City Tower
	One Raffles Quay
	One Raffles Link
	Raffles Museum of Biodiversity Research
	    (part of National University of Singapore
	    Science faculty)
	Raffles Park condominium

RAFFLES' STATUE	In front of Victoria Theatre and Concert Hall A replica erected at the mouth of the Singapore River to mark Raffles' landing site

THE BRITISH EAST INDIA COMPANY

The British East India Company was chartered by Queen Elizabeth I in 1600 and given a monopoly of trade between England and the Far East. Founded as the Company of Merchants of London Trading into the East Indies, it grew to dominate the commercial world of Asia and the Middle East.

Until its dissolution in 1874, trade in tea was the company's core business. In the late 18th and early 19th centuries, tea accounted for around half of the company's profits. It brought roughly 40,000 pounds of tea annually from China in the early 1700s, a figure that had risen to 26 million pounds by 1800. As the popularity of tea grew exponentially in Britain's domestic market, the company sought out a product that could be sold in the opposite direction. Several commodities were tried, but none found favour in the China market until the British hit on an export that generated its own demand: opium.

Opium had been banned in China since 1729. When it was reintroduced under pressure from the East India Company its use quickly spread. The East India Company was already producing opium in northern India, which was used as a popular medicine in Europe and elsewhere, and began shipping it to China as a means of offsetting the cost of importing Chinese tea. The China-India trade route became the company's most profitable, but every one of its ships had to pass through the narrow Malacca Straits, and to protect its interests, the company sought a base from which it could control the straits.

15

Collection of the KITLV, Leiden, The Netherlands

A seated portrait of a Chinese man in Singapore with an opium pipe, circa 1890.

16

The Mirror
OF
LITERATURE, AMUSEMENT, AND INSTRUCTION.

No. 599.]   SATURDAY, APRIL 13, 1833.   [Price 2*d*.

HET HUIS VAN 'DEN OOST INDISCHE COMPACNIE IN LON DEN

THE ORIGINAL EAST INDIA HOUSE, 1648.

EAST INDIA HOUSE, 1833.

The Mirror, the first long-lasting two-penny miscellany in Britain, said in 1833 the East India Company had been described "as the most celebrated commercial association, either of ancient or modern times, and which has now extended its sway over the whole of the Mogul empire." This Mirror cover shows, above, the company's original premises, occupied beginning in 1600 and once the house of the Lord Mayor of London, and, below, the company's new compound erected on the same site in the late 18th Century.

Historically, the Dutch were the principal colonial power in the region. From their capital at Batavia on Java they controlled an empire in the East Indies that stretched from New Guinea to the northern tip of Sumatra. The East India Company did not want to do anything to upset the Dutch on what the Dutch regarded as their own turf. Raffles had been told to proceed with the utmost discretion. He did not do as he was told. Instead, he forged ahead and set up a British trading post right under the noses of the Dutch.

News of what Raffles had done only reached his superior, the British Governor of Penang, John Bannerman, about two weeks after the fact. Bannerman, who neither liked nor trusted Raffles, urgently contacted the Dutch authorities in Batavia and assured them that Raffles had acted on his own initiative without the authority of the company.

The Dutch, who had considered using military force to drive the British out of Temasek, were pacified by assurances from Penang and by claims from Sultan Hussein that he had been intimidated by Raffles and had signed the treaty under duress. They decided to wait for the British to pull out, as Bannerman had assured them would happen.

Events in Singapore, however, were unfolding against the backdrop of a power shift across the globe. Britain had emerged from the Napoleonic wars as a major European power and as the undisputed maritime master of the world. Throughout the 18th century there had been ambivalence in London about the usefulness of colonies and about the best way in which they should be

17

"Whenever [Raffles] talked about furthering British ambitions east of Calcutta, everyone said, 'Oh, let's leave it as it is, don't rock the boat, you know. The Dutch aren't going to like it. And Raffles thought: 'Well, to hell with the Dutch! I like it, and I'm going to do it'. And he did!"
— Julian Davidson, author, *"One for the Road"*

By Courtesy of PSA Corporation Limited

A view of Singapore from the sea, 1837. Between 1822 and 1837 cargo handled in the port city increased fivefold.

18

administered. The empire had been acquired "by accident" and not everyone believed the accident had been fortuitous. But as the 19th century progressed, an assumption began to take hold in Britain: that its dominion over much of the world was the natural order of things. It had already become an article of faith in the corridors of the East India Company's headquarters. Bannerman's superiors did not concur with his view that the Dutch should be accommodated. They saw the strategic value of Singapore as a military and commercial base and instructed Bannerman to allow Raffles to stay put. To buy time, the British government added Singapore to the list of issues already under negotiation with the Dutch.

In 1824, under the Treaty of London, the Netherlands formally ceded control of Singapore to Britain, giving the force of law to the reality which Raffles' daring had created on the ground.

Singapore had become British because of the insubordination of a maverick and a visionary: if Raffles had followed the rules, if Bannerman had had his way, the history of Singapore—and the history of the whole of Southeast Asia—would have been very different.

The treaty, and international acquiescence in its provisions, represented a first step. Making Singapore a viable base was a greater challenge over the long term. Raffles realised that Singapore could not survive simply as a stopover point between India and China. It had to become self-sustaining, and that meant attracting traders who could turn the settlement into a thriving entrepôt.

The region was already peppered with small ports, and traders were scattered all across the archipelagoes of the South China Sea. Raffles needed to think of an incentive to lure traders to Singapore. His solution was conventional but effective: profit!

The steamer "Travancore" taking on cargo at Singapore, 1830.

"Raffles realised Singapore could become the centre for regional trade, and tap into the vast production base of the East Indies. Birds' nests from Borneo and camphor and resins from the jungle were used for lacquer, gold dust from Bali, and then of course, there's the main thoroughfare—the East/West trade route between China and India,"
— Julian Davidson, author, *"One for the Road"*

Singapore waterfront village, circa 1840.

Ships crowd the Singapore harbor, while docks in the foreground are laden with wares, circa 1890.

21

From its inception, Singapore's prosperity was based on free trade. The new British masters of the island understood that they could attract entrepreneurs if they guaranteed that they would not be subject to punitive taxation, and that their import-export operations would be completely tax-free. This guarantee set Singapore apart from competing ports in the region, and underpinned a period of exponential development.

With its free-trade credential in place, Singapore was poised to reap the advantage of the first wave of globalization. Ships, faster than before, flocked to the new city to load and unload cargo for global export.

Chapter 2

LIKE BEES TO HONEY

24

Rev. Thomas Raffles, cousin of Singapore founder Thomas Stanford Raffles, received frequent letters about the colony.

affles' big idea of free trade gathered merchants from the region to Singapore; as one contemporary said, "like bees to a honey pot". The place was swarming with commerce. Raffles saw that Singapore could be the centre for regional trade, tapping into the vast production bases of the East Indies.

In a letter to the Duke of Somerset, Raffles detailed the early successes of the colony. "My settlement of Singapore continues to prosper. By the returns of shipping and native vessels arrived since it has been in our possession, the following results appear: the total tonnage arrived in two years and a half has been upwards of 161,000 tons, and the estimated value of imports and exports 8,000,000 (Spanish) dollars or £2,000,000."

In another letter, to his cousin, Reverend Dr Thomas Raffles, he expressed his satisfaction at the development of Singapore four years after he established the colony.

"The progress of my new settlement is in every way most satisfactory. Every day brings us new settlers, and Singapore has already become a great emporium. Houses and warehouses are springing up in every direction, and the inland forests are fast giving way before the industrious cultivator."

While Raffles was delighted by this success, calling Singapore "his little child", he was, reluctantly, an absent father. On 28 June 1819 he sailed for Bencoolen, the remote British base in Southern Sumatra where, despite his recent foray to Singapore, he was still the governor. His duties in Bencoolen would keep Raffles away from Singapore for the next three and a half years.

Preceding page: Chinese smoking opium

Collection of the KITLV, Leiden, The Netherlands

Johnston Pier at One Fullerton, circa 1890. In the late 19th Century, Johnston Pier was one of the main arrival and departure points for passengers in Singapore.

25

During this time, the new settlement developed a life of its own. More and more people flocked to the island to enjoy the benefits of free trade. Chinese traders, who were already well established along the coast of the Malacca Straits, formed the bulk of the new arrivals. In time, more immigrants arrived from mainland China, driven overseas by the hardships faced at home because of misrule and poverty. Indians also came, some as traders and some as soldiers and civil servants already familiar with the ways of the British Empire. The Malay population on the island was originally made up mostly of fishermen and migrant sailors, but as Singapore's economy developed more settlers arrived from other parts of the Malay archipelago. In the four years after 1819, some 10,000 people established homes in Singapore.

National Archives of Singapore

Chinese Junk lying at anchor, Singapore, 1850.

The settlers enjoyed the benefits of free trade and the ability to devote themselves unhindered to the business of wealth creation. They also enjoyed religious freedom. From the very beginning, religious tolerance was part of the ethos of multi-ethnic Singapore. Modern Singaporeans still enjoy the same level of religious freedom as their forefathers did.

The different communities on the island preserved their traditions even as they integrated and became a single society. Many of the descendants of these early settlers still live in Singapore, making up the cultural smorgasbord that is Singapore today.

While he was away in Bencoolen, Raffles left Singapore in the care of William Farquhar. Farquhar, a Scotsman, had lived in the region for many years and had come to accept many of the local customs which Raffles, a relatively new arrival, still considered unacceptable. Slave trading, gambling and cock fighting were among the commonplace activities that Farquhar allowed. Even opium smoking, which had turned many of the Chinese workers into addicts, was not thwarted. Laws in the settlement were not enforced and people were generally left to do as they pleased. One consequence of this was rampant crime. Singapore was not growing up to be the proper little British child that Raffles has envisaged.

26

Collection of the KITLV, Leiden, The Netherlands

William Farquhar, who accompanied Raffles on his trip to Singapore in January 1918, was named first resident or administrator of the city, but had more interest in exploring the local flora than local moralities.

From the very beginning, religious tolerance was part of the ethos of multi-ethnic Singapore. Modern Singaporeans still enjoy the same level of religious freedom as their forefathers did.

"When Raffles returns in 1822, he is just aghast. It hasn't quite got the feel of the English colonial trade port that he imagined, and he basically fires Farquhar."

– Timothy Barnard, associate professor,
Department of History, National University of Singapore

27

By Courtesy of PSA Corporation Limited

A bustling road in Tanjong Pagar, circa 1894. The police station in the background was demolished in 1983 to make room for the expansion of Tanjong Pagar Container Terminal.

DR JOHN CRAWFURD

Writing to his cousin, Thomas Raffles, 10 days after leaving Singapore for the last time, Raffles noted that he had had "a great deal of trouble and annoyance in the details owing to the imbecility and obstinacy of the local Resident Colonel Farquhar." After dismissing Farquhar, Raffles appointed another Scotsman, Dr John Crawfurd, in his place. Crawfurd was a medical doctor, but had interests in languages, history and administration. He had joined the East India Company's medical service in 1803 at the age of 20 and had served in Penang and Java under Raffles. In 1821, he was sent as an envoy to Siam and Cochin-China (the south of what is now Vietnam) in an effort to open these areas to British trade. He was appointed resident of Singapore in June 1823.

Raffles and Farquhar left the island soon after Crawfurd took up his duties.

Crawfurd served from 1823 until 1826. Unlike Farquhar, he was instrumental in implementing key aspects of Raffles' original vision for Singapore. In particular, he signed treaties with the Dutch and the Malays solidifying Britain's possession of Singapore. He also focused on judicial and educational improvements. During Crawfurd's tenure as resident work began on implementing the master plan for the new city, which Raffles had drawn up on his return from Bencoolen in

Courtesy of National Museum of Singapore, National Heritage Board

John Crawfurd, Singapore's second resident, who implemented policies more attuned to Raffles' vision.

28

Getty Images

29

A bustling street scene in early Singapore.

1822. The Raffles Plan bears all the hallmarks of the Enlightenment. It is characterised by an enthusiastic belief in "progress", in the efficacy of trade and commerce and good government. It also displays a conviction that sensible town planning can alleviate many of society's ills.

Crawfurd departed for Britain in 1830 and never returned to the East, but he kept in contact with Singapore. In 1868, at the age of 85, Crawfurd became the first president of the Straits Settlements Association.

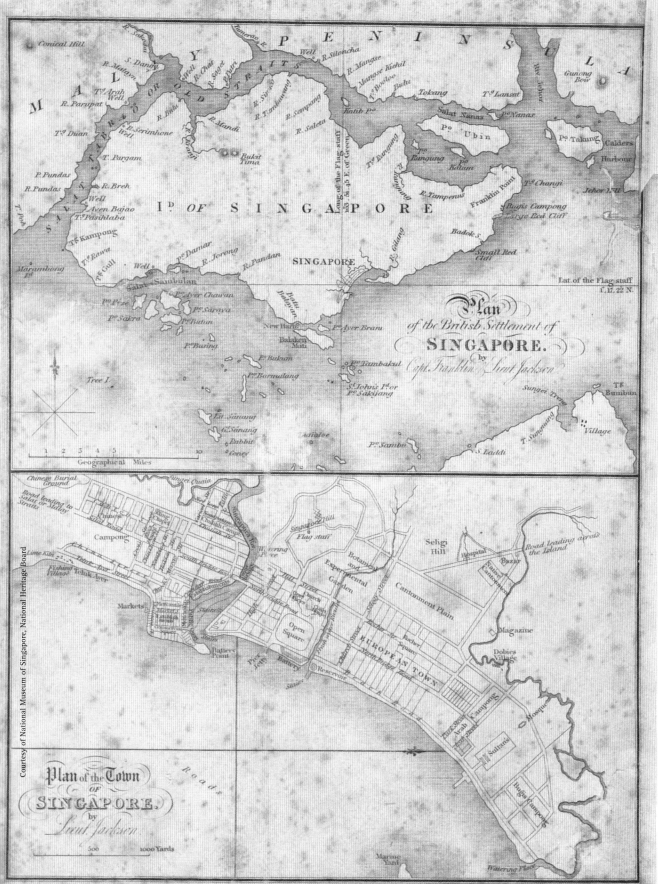

Plan
of the British Settlement of
SINGAPORE.
by
Capt. Franklin and Lieut. Jackson

Plan of the Town
OF
SINGAPORE.
by
Lieut. Jackson

Published by Henry Colburn, London, June 1828

THE TOWN PLAN OF 1822

Raffles' town plan clearly defined areas for different usage, and also separated the ethnic groups in Singapore. These areas are still present today.

THE RIVER AND QUAY

The Singapore River was to serve as the central artery of the town, the vibrant, bustling hub of a busy trading port. Tongkang, sampans and lightermen squeezed alongside one another, leaving barely enough room for larger sea craft. Sacks of rice and other merchandise were moved between the boats and the warehouses and godowns throughout the day. This was as Raffles had intended it to be. The plan provided for the creation of a wharf, Boat Quay, which would be the focal point of business on the river. Present day Boat Quay is lined with pubs and eateries rather than warehouses and godowns. The river today is quiet, with only the occasional passing pleasure boat to disturb its tranquility, but this stretch of water is the cradle of Singapore, the place where its rise to economic pre-eminence began.

Corbis Corporation

A view of the Singapore River and Boat Quay, 1950.

Preceding Page: Town plan for Singapore drawn by Lt. Philip Jackson, based on Raffles' aspirations, 1822.

COMMERCIAL SQUARE

An area of swampland southwest of the Singapore River was designated for commercial use. Close to the river a hill was leveled to become Commercial Square. This was in effect Singapore's first reclamation project. Unlike Boat Quay, the commercial area laid out in the 1822 plan still serves its original purpose and is very much the business hub that Raffles intended it to be. The central square in the business district has maintained the same dimensions and shape as in the original plan, though the surrounding cityscape has been utterly transformed. Today that square is known as Raffles Place.

Getty Images

Singapore Press Holdings

Raffles Place, the Mercantile Bank Building in the centre, 1951.

CHINATOWN

The Chinese population, made up mostly of traders, was concentrated close to the Singapore River, on the south side. The Chinese settled according to their home province, and were under the control of their respective chiefs, who maintained law and order. The Cantonese occupied Temple and Mosque Streets; the Hokkiens were located in Telok Ayer and Hokkien Streets, and the Teochews settled in South Canal Road, Garden Street and Carpenter Street.

The streets in Chinatown were laid out, as far as possible, on a rectilinear grid, which corresponded to 19th century ideas of good town planning. The plan also included detailed architectural prescriptions. For example, shophouses were to be brick-built and covered in tiles. Each shophouse had to have a verandah or covered passage five feet wide. This was to provide residents in the densely populated warren of streets with shade and fresh air.

Chinatown expanded in tandem with the expansion of the Chinese population. Before long, the Chinese spilled over to the northern side of the river, displacing the Europeans and Arabs. Today, the Chinese form the majority race, and are no longer confined to Chinatown!

Chinatown is now a heritage zone, where fine examples of brick shophouses and the "five-foot way" are preserved. The area, which is Singapore's largest historic district, bustles with activity during festivals such as Lunar New Year, attracting not just Chinese but other Singaporeans and visitors alike. In the late 1980s, four sub-districts—Bukit Pasoh, Kreta Ayer, Telok Ayer and Tanjong Pagar—were also granted conservation status, which has ensured that elements of their colourful past have been preserved too.

A street in Singapore's Chinatown.

33

KAMPONG GLAM

When Sultan Hussein ceded the island of Singapore to the British, Raffles promised to set aside an area specifically for the Sultan and his subjects.

A palace and mosque for the Sultan's use were to be built in this area, known today as Kampong Glam. The palace, Istana Kampong Glam, was built between 1840 and 1843 by Hussein's son, Sultan Ali Iskandah Shah, and was his residence till his death in 1891. A family succession dispute resulted in the estate being taken back by the British Crown in 1897 (and it became state land when Singapore gained her independence). Even so, descendants of the Sultan were allowed to live there till the early 1990s, when they were finally resettled to make way for conservation work. Today, the restored palace is the home of the Malay Heritage Centre, and Kampong Glam is a gazetted conservation district.

The first Sultan's mosque was built in 1826 in accordance with the 1824 Treaty of Friendship and Alliance signed by Sultan Hussein and John Crawfurd formally ceding the entire island of Singapore to the British (expanding on the terms of the 1819 treaty). Under the treaty, a sum of money was promised by the British East India Company to build a mosque in the Sultan's enclave. The present mosque was built in 1928 to accommodate the growing Muslim population. The mosque was designed by an Irishman, Denis Santry, employed by the architectural firm Swan and McLaren. In 1975 the Sultan Mosque was gazetted under the Preservation of Monuments Board Act.

National Archives of Singapore

ARAB STREET

Not far from Kampong Glam is Arab Street, allocated under the original plan to Arab traders who sold textiles and spices there. Over time, the Arab merchants were joined by Indian Muslim traders, who also sold textiles and jewellery in Arab Street. Today, visitors to Kampong Glam and Arab Street will find a range of traditional shops selling the merchandise that has been a staple of this area for almost two centuries. East of Kampong Glam was a district allocated to the Bugis, a sea-faring people from South Sulawesi in Indonesia.

Arab Street shophouses, 1963.

LITTLE INDIA

The Raffles plan allocated a tract along the southern banks for Singapore River as the Indian enclave. But Indian soldiers and bureaucrats versed in the ways of the British, as well as traders and convicts, quickly arrived in greater numbers than the enclave could house. The immigrant Indians established a new concentration around Serangoon River.

While modern Singapore housing policies deter ethnic enclaves, the Indian settlements have evolved into "Little India," focused along Serangoon Road. The tourist destination features shop fronts selling textiles, saris and other Indian merchandise, as well as a wide range of Indian cuisine. Little India is the heart of Indian festivals in Singapore, and includes the ornate Sri Veeramakaliamman Temple, which was built by immigrants from Bengal in 1881.

36

National Archives of Singapore

*Flower garland stall along
Campbell Road at Little India*

EUROPEAN ENCLAVE

The plan provided for a "European Town" in the Beach Road area between Stamford Canal and Arab Street, where the iconic Raffles Hotel was later built. The European settlement, however, expanded into the Claymore and Tanglin areas, Orchard Road and River Valley, as well as Telok Blangah.

The fact that parts of Singapore today still reflect the use they were allocated under the original plan is testimony to Raffles' remarkable foresight. Shortly before leaving Singapore he wrote that he had introduced a "system of energy, purity, and encouragement that will last for a century or two".

And he was right.

One little known fact is that Raffles spent a total of just nine months in Singapore. But in that short time he managed to transform it from an obscure Malay fishing village into a bustling port that had begun to act as a magnet for settlers from elsewhere in the region and beyond. Raffles arrived back in Britain in August 1823. He died three years later of a suspected brain tumour.

Roger-Viollet/AFP

Ox-carts on Singapore streets, 1900.

37

DEATH OF SIR STAMFORD RAFFLES

Raffles died at his home in Highwood on 5 July 1826, on the eve of his 45th birthday. Marking his death, *The Gentleman's* Magazine of London wrote:

"He had passed the preceding day [of his death] in the bosom of his family, and, excepting a bilious attack under which he had laboured for some days, there was nothing in his appearance to create the least apprehension that the fatal hour was so near. Sir Stamford had retired to rest on the Tuesday evening [4th July] between ten and eleven o'clock, his usual hour when in the country. On the following morning at five o'clock, it being discovered that he had left his room before the time at which he generally rose, six o'clock, Lady Raffles immediately rose, and found him lying at the bottom of a flight of stairs in a state of complete insensibility. Medical aid was promptly procured, and every means resorted to, to restore animation, but the vital spark had fled. The body was opened, under the direction of Sir Everard Home, the same day, who pronounced his death to have been caused by an apoplectic attack, beyond the control of all human power. It was likewise apparent that the sufferings of the deceased, must, for some time past, have been most intense."

He is buried at St Mary's Church in Hendon, where a brass tablet erected by the Reverend R.B. Raffles, bears the following inscription:

In Memory of Sir Thomas Stamford Raffles, F.R.S., LL.D.,
Statesman, Administrator, and Naturalist,
Founder of the colony and city of Singapore, 29th January 1819;
Born 5 July 1781, died at Highwood, Middlesex,
July 5th, 1826, and buried near this tablet.
Erected in 1887 by members of the family.

38

Frederick Pearl (left), British MP and Lord President of the Privy Council, delivers to Singapore the first volume of a set of letters written by Stamford Raffles, August 1969.

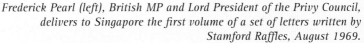

By 1887, fortunes were being made in Singapore. More than half a century of free trade policies had created a prosperous and cosmopolitan community of traders and merchants. Businessmen like Hoo Ah Kay were building commercial empires on the back of the city's *laissez-faire* economics.

Hoo, better known as Whampoa—a variation of Huangpo, his birthplace in Canton—came to Singapore when he was 15 years old to work in his father's provisions shop, Whampoa & Co. Whampoa inherited the business after his father's death, and his commercial know-how and English fluency gave him an edge over competitors. Whampoa could buy and sell almost anything.

Whampoa was popular with the British and moved effortlessly among the highest social circles, which helped him, for instance, become a ship chandler for the Royal British Navy. The British called him "the best Chinaman who ever lived," and he was well-known for his lavish dinners and the splendid Whampao Garden. Among his lasting contributions to the city were the gardens, which became part of Singapore Botanic Gardens when he exchanged them with the city for warehouse property on Boat Quay, the Singapore River's bustling dockside.

Traders in Singapore found it easy to create wealth—they operated without the burden of customs duties or corporate tax. However, the East India Company, which ran the colony, fared less well. In the mid 19th century the company's administrative capacity was overstretched; at the same time, faced with major changes in global trading patterns and the rise of new competitors, its income slumped.

40

By Courtesy of PSA Corporation Limited

"The kind of people who were getting really rich were the local traders. They were Chinese, and they were Arabs, and they were Indians who were operating what in today's terms you would call small and medium enterprises."

– Wang Gung Wu, director, East Asian Institute

"It wasn't bringing any profit or interest to the Company whatsoever. The private merchants were making a great deal of money, but none of this was getting into the government coffers."
– Mary Turnbull, author, *"A History of Singapore"*

Merchant offices and godowns, or warehouses, line Collyer Quay, circa 1870.

The East India Company was losing interest in Raffles' little child, which had increasingly come to be viewed by the company as more burden than asset.

As a result of administrative neglect by the company, public services in Singapore, such as policing, began to suffer. Money was not forthcoming for necessary infrastructure maintenance, such as improvements to the port. Free trade was making individual residents of Singapore wealthy, but it was not providing for the general welfare of the settlement.

With no revenue from income tax, company taxes, or customs duties, the British sought alternative methods of funding for the settlement. Their solution was eminently practical, if morally dubious: opium.

The authorities began issuing licenses for the right to sell opium in Singapore. These licenses were sold at auction; once they had secured a license, traders were able to sell the drug freely. Since many Chinese in Singapore were already addicted to opium, dealing in the drug was an avenue to quick wealth. In 1824, an opium farm rented at $1,925 per month; by 1841, the monthly rental had risen to $6,250. Opium farms continued to increase in value for the rest of the century.

Around the turn of the century, the Straits Settlements, which included Singapore, Penang and Malacca, raised a good portion of its revenues from opium, violence linked to the trade often spilled into the streets.

41

OPIUM TRADE IN SINGAPORE

From the mid-1800s until the early 20th century, opium was a significant element of the commercial scene in Singapore. Since it was used in barter for local produce, its price affected the value of all other commodities. Opium also developed as the link connecting the colonial British administrators with the local Chinese population. The opium farm has been described by author Carl Trocki as the "Chinese power centre of the colony". As in many other countries at the time, in the absence of adequate supplies of silver, opium served as an alternative currency.

Opium was used to treat a range of illnesses such as asthma, cancer, catarrh, cold, conjunctivitis, cough, diarrhoea, dysmenorrhoea, fever, hypertension, hysteria, insomnia, malaria, melancholy, nausea, rheumatism and even snakebites, apart from pain-related illnesses such as stomachache, swelling and toothache. It was also consumed in liquid form, as laudanum, and smoked for its narcotic effect. Among the leisured classes it was a recreational drug, while for the poor it was a means of blotting out the relentless misery of daily life.

The practice was brought to Singapore by Chinese migrants; in 1848 there were an estimated 15,000 opium smokers in the settlement, mostly poor and elderly coolies. The prevalence of opium smoking led to a spike in crime, as addicts resorted to stealing and abduction to support their habit.

In 1907, the colonial government appointed a Opium Commission to "enquire into matters relating to the use of opium in the Straits Settlements". The commission met more than 50 times and its investigation covered not just Singapore but Penang, Taiping, Ipoh and Kuala Lumpur.

National Archives of Singapore

The Opium Commission of the Straits Settlements in Federated Malay States, 1907-1908.

Among its conclusions were that Chinese women and boys under the age of 15 and non-Chinese scarcely smoked at all, and that per capita opium consumption in 1907 had fallen from the level reached a decade earlier.

The commission also concluded that the physical effect of "moderate smoking" was relatively mild. It recommended that the government take full charge of the manufacture and distribution of opium in order to prevent adulteration and fraud. It also recommended that the number of retail outlets selling opium be reduced and that the acquisition of opium by women and children be made as difficult as possible. Among other things, it suggested that the price of opium be increased.

Opium dens were concentrated in the Chinatown area, in Pagoda Street and Trengganu Street. Tanjong Pagar and the Rochor areas around Sungei Road. Duxton Road, Amoy Street and Beach Road were also popular for opium dens as late as the 1970s. Opium was formally banned in Singapore in 1943 during the Japanese occupation, and the ban was maintained after the resumption of British rule in 1945. Still, the opium trade continued through illegal trafficking, and in 1989 Singapore introduced the death penalty for opium dealers in a renewed effort to curb the market.

Collection of the KITLV, Leiden, The Netherlands

"Behind the windows of shop houses were opium dens and brothels. The British tolerated these squalid establishments because they generated revenue which enabled the company to govern Singapore."
– Tan Tai Yong, dean, Faculty of Arts and Social Sciences, National University of Singapore

44

Opium was not the only dubious means of raising revenue encouraged by the East India Company. The company also sanctioned international human trafficking, a business that was particularly lucrative in Singapore where for much of the 19th century the male population hugely outnumbered the female population. Prostitution was big business. The free-flowing vice of the period gave the island the dubious moniker "Sin-Galore" among the locals.

The opium dens and brothels were run mostly by secret societies, powerful, clan-based organisations with complex roots in mainland China. They had a grip on anyone who patronised their businesses—rickshaw drivers, shopkeepers, traders, police officers and individuals from practically every walk of life. This gave them enormous power and undermined in a visible way the concept of law and order in the settlement, as rival gangs engaged in pitched battles over profits and territory.

The secret societies made a fetish of loyalty—members were expected to defend the honour of their clan against anyone who tried to interfere with their lucrative business. Finding the gang hierarchies and membership structures too complex to penetrate, the British were totally unable to bring them under control, so they turned to their own favourites in the Chinese community, men such as Hoo Ah Kay. Yet many of the individuals whom the British sought to use as instruments for controlling in the power of the secret societies were themselves connected to the gangs, which meant that inadvertently the British had created a vicious connection between opium, crime and the Chinese community as a whole. By the time they realised this, it was almost too late to remedy the situation.

Singapore, which had built a reputation as a major centre of trade, began to develop a parallel and infinitely less positive reputation as a centre of sleaze. The British appeared to have neither the will nor the means to change this.

Fortunately for Singapore, change did come, not from within, but as the result of an event that took place thousands of miles away in Egypt.

The Thian Hock Keng temple in Singapore, circa 1890. Chinese Hokkien immigrants visited the temple to give thanks to Ma Zu, the goddess of the sea. Begun in 1839, the temple also held the offices and meetings rooms for the Hokkien clan.

45

Chapter 3

FORTUNES

48

While Singapore's administrators were struggling to raise money while preserving the city's free-trade reputation, the city's merchants and traders were thriving. And during the second half of the 19th Century, businesses received substantial boosts from events far from the island's shores.

The Suez Canal opened in 1869 and changed the structure of trade between Europe and Asia forever. Before the Canal opened, European ships bound for the Far East had to take a circuitous route around the Cape of Good Hope at the southern tip of Africa. After 1869 they were able to sail from the Mediterranean directly into the Indian Ocean and then down the Malacca Straits to Singapore and onward to China and other parts of East Asia. The canal cut 5,000 miles from the journey, and in the five years after it opened, trade between Europe and Asia increased by 50 per cent.

The opening of the Suez Canal breathed new life into Singapore. It also signalled the start of Singapore's development as a hub of Southeast Asia. Previously the colony had served primarily as a port of call for ships bound for China; now it became the first port of call for any Western ship operating in the region. Singapore received the boost that it needed badly at the time. Ships from the West would unload their cargos in Singapore, and these wares would be divided into smaller lots and routed to their final destinations.

Next, less than 10 years after the opening of the Suez Canal, Singapore's fortunes received another boost, this time from Brazil.

Preceding page: Rubber plantation

"If ships were to come from London and distribute various products, it would be more economical [for them] to come to a centre, and from that centre, break [the goods] into smaller parcels and distribute them to various parts of Southeast Asia. This is the concept of the hub."
– Lim Chong Yah, professor of economics,
Nanyang Technological University

49

Experts inspect a rubber tree on a plantation.

By the middle of the 19th century, Brazil accounted for as much as 90 per cent of the world's supply of natural rubber. To maintain this dominant position the Brazilian authorities went to considerable lengths to prevent rubber seeds from being taken out of the country. By 1853, British inventor, Thomas Hancock, had developed a method

National Archives of Singapore

*A Singapore Malay boy tapping
a rubber tree using a method
Henry Ridley pioneered, 1920.*

for using rubber in industrial production. He and, Scotsman Charles Macintosh began producing waterproof raincoats. The two approached the Royal Botanic Gardens at Kew in London and suggested that they grow rubber plants themselves. But it wasn't until June 1876 that Sir Henry Wickham was able to smuggle 70,000 rubber seeds out of Brazil and take them to Kew Gardens. A small proportion of the seeds were successfully nursed into plants, and in 1877, several saplings were sent from Kew to the Botanic Gardens in Singapore.

The export of rubber saplings to Southeast Asia might have had very little impact had it not been for the work of Henry Ridley, who became director of the Singapore Botanic Gardens in 1888. Ridley had travelled to Brazil the year before his appointment in Singapore and recognised that rubber was ideally suited to the climate of Southeast asia. He quickly embarked on a zealous mission to promote its cultivation.

"The story went that whenever he went to a function, he would take some rubber seeds and put them into other guests' pockets. Later on, some people thought he went a bit cuckoo, and they called him Mad Ridley. But he was not mad. History proved that he was right."
– Lim Chong Yah, professor of economics,
Nanyang Technological University

SIR HENRY NICHOLAS RIDLEY

Sir Henry Nicholas Ridley, was a botanist, geologist and the first Scientific director of the Singapore Botanic Gardens, serving from 1888 to 1911. Ridley is generally credited with establishing the rubber industry in the Malay Peninsula and turning Malaya into the world's number one rubber producer.

When rubber saplings first arrived in Singapore, local planters showed scant interest in a crop that took six or seven years to start generating income. It was only Ridley's near fanatical enthusiasm that persuaded a small number of planters to begin experimenting with the plant. Soon after he arrived in Singapore in 1888, he ordered the earth around the existing rubber trees at the Botanic Gardens to be cleared and planted with additional seeds; he then set about developing new ways of tapping rubber. In 1895 he perfected a method whereby a "V" shape was cut into the tree and the rubber sap allowed to drip into a cup tied to the trunk. This technique, which had the merit of inflicting no permanent damage to the tree, is still used in rubber plantations today.

Ridley retired from Singapore in 1911 and returned to Britain, where he continued his work as a researcher and writer, living close to the Botanic Gardens at Kew. He died in 1956 just a few months before his 101st birthday.

With his enthusiasm and his technical breakthrough, Ridley single-handedly launched a commercial revolution that changed the commercial landscape of Southeast Asia and had a major impact all across the globe. Rubber made fortunes and was often called "white gold."

It wasn't until 1907 that the first rubber trees were grown commercially in Singapore, at Trafalgar Coconut Plantation in Ponggol. But Singapore did not have the necessary land area to grow rubber trees in the quantity that would meet global demand. Ridley had prepared the way for a commercial rubber industry just in time for the huge increase in demand spawned by the exponential growth of the fledgling automobile industry. In the early years of the 20th century, Singapore planters began moving into Malaya, where they established huge rubber estates.

In 1911, the Singapore Chamber of Commerce established a Rubber Association, whose primary purpose as to hold auctions for rubber. While much of the rubber was still sold between these auctions, the auction region's set a transparent price for the commodity and helped create a stable market. This encouraged a growing number of rubber brokers to sell their stock in Singapore. In 1918, the 51,200 tons brought for auction in Singapore represented nearly one quarter of world exports.

Because of Singapore's growing importance as the centre of the world rubber trade, Japanese, Americans and Europeans began flocking to the city. Three large American corporations —the United States Rubber Company, Firestone and Goodyear— established offices in Singapore to purchase the raw material.

National Archives of Singapore

Singapore Rubber Association Representative Press Conference

THE RUBBER BARONS

By introducing rubber to Southeast Asia, Henry Ridley laid the groundwork for great family empires. One of the first successful rubber entrepreneurs was Tan Kah Kee, an immigrant from Fujian province who would later be known as the "Rubber King."

Also known as the "Henry Ford of Malaya," Tan was a penniless 17-year-old in 1890 when he arrived in Singapore to help with his father's rice shop. After the business failed in 1903, possibly as a result of embezzlement by a relative, Tan established a small pineapple cannery and later expanded by building a rice mill. His success soared, however, after he converted the rice mill into a rubber mill, later founding Sumbawa Rubber Manufacturer, which made rubber goods ranging from toys to tyres. At the peak of his success, his empire spread from Thailand to China and, along with rubber, included sawmills real estate, import- and export-brokerages and shipping.

Tan was also known as a generous philanthropist who built schools in Singapore and Fujian, China, including the Chinese High School in Singapore (today called Hwa Chong Institution) and Xiamen University in China.

53

Singapore Press Holdings

Tan Kah Kee founded a number of schools in Singapore and in his birthplace, China.

David Ng, courtesy of National Archives of Singapore

Lee Kong Chian

54

A leader of the Hokkien community in Singapore and chairman of the Chinese Chamber of Commerce, Tan advocated social reform and opposed gambling and opium, both wide-spread in the Chinese community. Tan was an active supporter of the Chinese Communist Party and settled into various party roles in China in his later life when the British refused him re-entry into Singapore because of his activities during the Chinese Revolution.

Another prominent Singapore rubber baron was Lee Kong Chian, who was closely connected to Tan. Lee came to Singapore in 1904 at the age of 10, also from Fujian. In 1917, Tan needed a trusted English speaker and hired Lee to manage his rubber company's expansion in North America and Europe. Linking the pair even closer, Lee married Tan's daughter, Tan Ai Leh, in 1920.

Lee did started his own business in 1927. He renamed the Lee Smoke House in Johor, the Lee Rubber Company and relocated the operation the following year to an abandoned factory in Singapore. Tan had by then moved out of rubber processing and into manufacturing so Lee was able to continue working with his father-in-law while managing his own business.

The Lee Rubber Company began as a partnership between Lee Kong Chian and his friends Lee Pee Soo and Yap Geok Tui, although Lee Kong Chian himself ran the business.

Lee expanded the company quickly and aggressively, venturing into industries other than rubber. He set up several business operations in Malaya, including the Lian Hin Group. By 1939, he had also established separate companies in Indonesia (Hok Tong Group), and Thailand (Siam Pakthai). The South Asia Corporation was established in New York in 1938 to handle the export of rubber to the United States. Lee had also started accumulating rubber estates in Malaya. Besides rubber, Lee expanded into pineapple planting and biscuit manufacturing. These businesses were operated under subsidiaries of Lee Rubber—Lee Pineapple and Lee Biscuit. After the war, the group diversified into sundry shops, tractor leasing, sawmills and coconut oil refinery operations among other things. The sawmill business was a natural offshoot of the pineapple operation— when forest was cleared to grow pineapples, the company had to dispose of the timber.

Eventually Lee and his partners went into the banking business. In 1932, when the Chinese Commercial Bank amalgamated with the Ho Hong Bank and the Oversea-Chinese Bank to form the Oversea-Chinese Banking Corporation (OCBC), Lee played an active role in the merger negotiations. He was appointed Chairman of OCBC when it was formed, even though he held only a small share of the bank's equity. After the war, he became the largest shareholder and his family today holds a stake of around 20 per cent in OCBC.

Rubber was not the only source of precipitous wealth creation in Singapore and Malaya during the 19th and 20th centuries. Another major staple of economic growth was tin. The popularity of canned food from the mid-19th century onwards created a rising demand for the raw material. Tin mining operations began in Malaya in the 1820s and quickly attracted a mainly Chinese labour force to the states of Perak, Sungei Ujong and Selangor. Foreign investment, mostly British and Chinese, funded the industry. After Britain expanded its direct control into the tin mining states in 1874, the industry became increasingly mechanised. Exports of tin from Malaya rose from 26,000 tons in 1889 to 51,733 tons in 1904 and just under 70,000 tons in 1929. By the 1920s Malaya accounted for more than half of the world's output of tin.

56

In order to prevent the loss of a significant portion of the value-add in the tin-making process, the British authorities placed an export duty on tin ore. This made it more profitable to complete the smelting process in Malaya or Singapore than to send the ore to other countries for smelting. As a result, Singapore, which already had advanced port facilities to ship the finished product to overseas markets, became the world's biggest tin-smelting centre. Not only did Singapore receive tin ore for smelting from Malaya, but also from Siam, French Indo-China, Burma, Australia, China, and Central and South Africa.

Malaya thus became the natural and economic hinterland of Singapore, and the two developed as an integrated, thriving economic unit.

Getty Images

The Sungei Besi Mine, a dry-excavated open cast tin mine, near Kuala Lumpur, Selangor, Malaysia, 1957.

National Archives of Singapore

By the middle of the 19th century it was clear that the government and administration of Singapore had failed to keep up with the island's economic development and demographic expansion. Law enforcement was minimal, and much of the city was controlled by secret Chinese societies. Robberies and murders were almost daily occurences.

The East India Company lost its monopoly on trade in 1833, and as a result it quickly lost interest in Singapore and Southeast Asia. Administration of the Straits Settlements was transferred to the governor-general of India in 1851. The company's power weakened further following 1857 Indian Mutiny, which spread violence throughout northern India and posed a serious threat to British rule. In the aftermath of the uprising, the British Crown took over administration of India. Calcutta, the capital of India during the British Raj, had little interest in Singapore and saw the small colony as a peripheral responsibility.

57

Singapore - opening of a new dock, 1869.

"The new governors were not just businessmen anymore. They were graduates of Oxford and Cambridge—they were people with a mission. It was an imperial mission to offer the people the best of British civilisation."
– Wang Gung Wu, director, East Asian Institute

Over the years, the mostly British business community in Singapore began to feel neglected by the Calcutta government and started lobbying for direct rule from London. Examples of inefficiencies in the existing arrangement included long delays in correspondence between London and Singapore, which had to be processed through the bureaucracy in Calcutta. It was also pointed out that the Straits Settlements had no voice in the Indian legislative council. Other complaints concerned the East India Company's attempt to make the *rupee* legal tender in the Straits Settlements, and what was perceived as a company policy of using Singapore as a "dumping ground" for Indian convicts. Beginning in 1825, the British government shipped Indian convicts to Singapore. By 1845, an estimated 1,500 Indian convicts has been bought to Singapore.

After ten years of petitioning, the Straits Settlements were finally transferred to the direct rule of the British Crown, on 1 April 1867, and Sir Harry St George Ord became the first governor, with his official seat in Singapore.

Distancing itself from the years of lawlessness and neglect, Singapore now embarked on a period of consolidation and development as a settled, prosperous and law-abiding society. The *laissez-faire* administration of the East India Company was replaced by cohorts of professional civil servants imbued with a sense of Victorian morality.

"Once Singapore was acknowledged as a British colony, investing in good government became necessary," explained Wang Gung Wu, director of the East Asia Institute at the National University of Singapore and author of several books about China and Southeast Asia. "The British government had to protect its reputation as having a good

Collection of the KITLV, Leiden, The Netherlands

A tailor shop in Chinatown, circa 1890.

58

legal system, and Singapore also had to remain attractive so that more traders and businessmen would invest and use Singapore as a base for their businesses."

Among other things, the colony began to benefit from British Government funding. After years of neglect, new roads and public buildings were constructed. Facilities established in this period included law courts and a police station.

The new crop of British officials recognised the importance of understanding and interacting with the island's Chinese elite, and many of them learned to read and speak Chinese, so that at last the island's colonial rulers began to use the language of the people they ruled.

"The new governors were not just businessmen anymore," Wang told Discovery Channel. "They were graduates of Oxford and Cambridge. They were people with a mission. It was an imperial mission to offer the people the best of British civilisation."

59

Collection of the KITLV, Leiden,
The Netherlands

*A Chinese street in Singapore
decorated for the visit of Prince Albert,
husband of Queen Victoria, 1860.*

"Once Singapore was acknowledged as a British Crown colony, investing in good government became necessary.

– Wang Gung Wu, director, East Asian Institute

A well-known brothel at Smith and Trengganu streets in Singapore, circa 1910. Brothels, often operating out of tea houses, were common in the area.

60

The new administration immediately set about the long overdue task of cleaning up corruption, ending forced prostitution and curbing the power and influence of the secret societies. The government of the Crown Colony was able to tackle these and other issues more effectively as a result of having direct access to the Colonial Office in London, to which it could appeal for funding and other resources.

The new colonial administration discouraged the use of opium, in marked contrast to the policy of the company, which had directly benefited from the opium trade. In addition, the authorities sought to regulate prostitution and instituted a complete ban on the secret societies. In order to continue operating and trading in Singapore, Chinese businessmen such as Whampoa were made to disavow their links with the criminal underworld. In turn they were invited to become part of the colonial establishment. Whampoa himself became the only Chinese to hold the post of extraordinary member in the Executive Legislative Council. Singapore would never again have the characteristics of a "Wild East" frontier town.

In 1887, to mark Queen Victoria's Golden Jubilee, a statue was erected honouring the city's founder, Sir Stamford Raffles. Also in that year, the now famous hotel bearing his name opened. Raffles Hotel came to represent the epitome of colonial sophistication in the East.

Straits Settlements Legislative Council members, 1873.

RAFFLES HOTEL

The Raffles Hotel, famous the world over as the birthplace of the Singapore Sling, was founded in 1887 by four Armenian brothers—Tigran, Arshak, Martin and Aviet Sarkies—who were combing the area for a site for a new hotel. The brothers, already owners of the Eastern and Oriental Hotel in Penang, were looking to diversify their holdings following a rent increase in Penang. In Singapore, they found a site on prestigious Twenty-House Street (today's Beach Road) known as the George Julius Dare Mansion being run as a *tiffin* room or lunch room.

Raffles Hotel, Singapore

Joe Constantine, Tigran Sarkies, Martin Sarkies and Martyrose Sarkies Arathoon (left to right) in a portrait soon after the Raffles Hotel opened, 1906. Constantine and Arathoon were executives in the Sarkies brothers' hotel business.

61

62

Raffles Hotel, Singapore

Raffles Hotel facade 1921. Raffles established itself as the preferred Singapore hotel of the rich and famous.

The Sarkies brothers leased the property from a local Arab trader, Syed Mohamed Alsagoff, and opened the Raffles Hotel in December 1887. Named after Singapore's founding father, the hotel that would eventually define luxury for many Singaporeans began as a simple three-story building with 10 guest rooms. In later years, the brothers would also open hotels in Indonesia and Burma.

The hotel quickly became famous, and celebrities of the time graced its guest list. Joseph Conrad is said to have conceived "Lord Jim" while staying at Raffles Hotel in 1897. Two years later, Rudyard Kipling, more impressed by the food and ambience than by the rooms, advised visitors to Singapore to "Feed at Raffles, but stay elsewhere", an ambivalent endorsement which the hotel's management put to imaginative use simply by lopping off second phrase and inserting the first part into its publicity material. Other celebrated writers who stayed at Raffles included Herman Hesse, Andre Malraux, Pablo Neruda, James Michener, Somerset Maugham and Noël Coward.

Over the years, the hotel was enlarged, with the addition of the Palm Court wing and what is now the main building. The hotel's grandeur was underscored by its elegant neo-Renaissance architecture and grand spaces. It boasted Singapore's first electric lights and fans, and a French chef.

Raffles became one of the city's premier social venues, hosting dinner dances, skating dinners and billiard competitions. In August 1902, according to legend, the last tiger to be killed in Singapore was shot, while cowering under a table in the Bar & Billiard Room, then an elevated building.

Some time between 1910 and 1915, Raffles Hotel's bartender Ngiam Tong Boon created the Million Dollar Cocktail and the Singapore Sling. The latter has since grown to become a cocktail of legendary proportions, served in bars and pubs around the world after its invention at Raffles Hotel.

The Raffles established itself as the preferred Singapore hotel of the rich and famous, and cinema idols who stayed there included Charlie Chaplin, Maurice Chevalier, Jean Harlow, Ava Gardner and Elizabeth Taylor. However, the hotel's financial performance was less impressive than its reputation as a celebrity hangout. By the 1930s, the Great Depression and a drop in Malay rubber trading were taking their toll. In 1931, the year the last of the four Sarkies brothers, Arshak, died, the family business, including Raffles Hotel and the Eastern & Oriental Hotel, went into receivership. The business was relaunched in 1933 when it was taken over by a new company called Raffles Hotel Ltd.

After the Japanese surrendered to the Allied Forces and Singapore returned to British control in 1945, Raffles Hotel became a temporary transit camp for liberated prisoners of war. By then the hotel, once a byword for sophistication, was a shadow of its former self.

Once reopened as a hotel, Raffles again became a stopover for celebrities. The hotel was the setting for at least two films. In 1967, "Pretty Polly," starring Trevor Howard and Hayley Mills and directed by Guy Green, was filmed there, as was "Raffles Hotel," a 1989 production by Japanese director Ryu Murakami.

Raffles Hotel was designated a national monument in 1987. The hotel was closed in 1989 for an extensive S$160 million renovation intended to revive the hotel's ambiance from its heyday in 1915. It reopened in 1991.

"If he had been there to witness the unveiling of his own statue, I think he would have been largely very pleased with what he saw. The prosperity of the place, the fact that it was this great hub of trade, the general freedom that people had to live as they liked—that would have pleased him too."

– Mary Turnbull, author, *"A History of Singapore"*

National Archives of Singapore

Raffles statue was unveiled on Jubilee Day, 27 June 1887.

B y the time the British Empire celebrated the Golden Jubilee of Queen Victoria's reign, Raffles had been dead for more than 60 years, but his little child had come of age, and his name would forever be associated with the fortunes of the colony.

Singapore marked the Golden Jubilee in 1887 with the unveiling of a statute of Raffles, the British explorer who had become a local icon. "If he (Raffles) had been there to witness the unveiling of his own statue, I think he would have been largely very pleased with what he saw," remarked Mary Turnbull, a noted historian of Southeast Asia and author of *A History of Singapore.* The prosperity of the place, the fact that it was this great hub of trade, the general freedom that people had to live as they liked—that would have pleased him, too."

But if Raffles is the icon of Singapore's colonial development, the city would soon have a native son who would become synonymous with the city's emergence as a modern economic powerhouse. Like Raffles, Harry Lee Kuan Yew would have a vision for this island off the southern tip of continental Asia, and, like Raffles, Lee would have to challenge forces beyond its shores to bring that vision forward.

"It is refreshing in some ways, in this anti-colonial age, that you get not only the acceptance of this figure but almost a glorification. Singaporeans often seem to think that their founder was a lily-white god almost."

— Mary Turnbull, author, *A History of Singapore*

James Song, courtesy of National Archives of Singapore

*View of Cavenagh Bridge &
Victoria Memorial Hall, 1890.*

Lee, born in 1923, would be country's first prime minister and set the foundation for modern Singapore. But Lee would not forget the country's debt to Raffles or its colonial roots. As prime minister, one of his early decisions was to ensure that the statue of Raffles erected on Jubilee Day would remain in the centre of the city. A second statue of Raffles, moulded from the original bronze statue, would be erected in 1972 to mark the location of Raffles' first landing.

"The legacy is that of connectedness with the world," Lee told Discovery Channel. "That was what made Singapore get off the ground. From a barely inhabited island, infertile, of no consequence to the world, he [Raffles] made it an important hub, and that we must keep up because otherwise, we would sink back to a fishing village."

With a population comprising Chinese from various parts of China, Indians from various parts of India, and Malays from various parts of the archipelago, Lee's challenge was to weld the country's citizens into single cohesive society so that Singapore would become their home, and not just a transit point. "I had to make this place work," Lee said.

Singapore's journey from colony to nationhood continues. The country is still young, but at every twist and turn, the impact of Sir Thomas Stamford Raffles has been felt. He created a trading post in the jungle and gave birth to a modern city.

Lim Chong Yah, director of the Economic Growth Centre at Nanyang Technological University in Singapore, noted, "One of these foundations that has never changed since Raffles set it in motion was free trade. This principle was upheld by the British government and the independent Singapore government throughout."

67

ACCIDENTAL NATION

Chapter 4

A POLITICAL AWAKENING

72

The 20th Century would witness wide-ranging and surprising changes for Raffles' Southeast Asian colony. It would force Singaporeans to choose among various allegiances. It would test their mettle under a brutal occupation. And it would see—perhaps for the first time in history—a prime minister weep in anguish as his country is handed, almost forcefully, complete independence.

After almost 100 years as a relatively serene British colony, events in other parts of the world would jostle and break the island's peacefulness. Raffles' little child would have a difficult adolescence.

As the 1900s began to unfold, Singapore, like many parts of the world, was enjoying a period of prosperity. In the 80 years since the Union Jack was raised, Singapore had become a valuable outpost for the British Empire; its port the seventh busiest in the world. No longer a swampy backwater, Singapore had grown into a major metropolis.

The architects of Singapore's success were the British, and consequently their right to rule was not questioned. Local business and community leaders enthusiastically helped the British with the day-to-day running of the colony.

Many well-established Malay, Indian and Chinese families had worked with the British for generations.

In July, 1901, some of these wealthy and well-connected locals were invited to Singapore's town hall for a notable event, the screening of the first ever ciné film to be shown on the island. The film included footage from the funeral of Queen Victoria, who had died in January after a reign of more than 63 years.

Preceding page: Group photograph of the members of The Straits Chinese Association with Dr Lim Boon Keng (in the centre)

Singapore and the Singapore River seen from Government Hill, 1850.

"They were very happy to be of service because they had neither nationalistic ideals, nor aspirations to leadership. It was a very comfortable relationship."

– Wang Gung Wu, Director, East Asian Institute

74

Yet even as Singapore's wealthy and influential citizens watched moving pictures of emperors, kings and princes following Victoria's cortege through the crowded streets of London, a major shift was taking place in their own society that few had yet to understand.

In the streets of Singapore, far removed from the respectable precincts of the town hall, hundreds of thousands of immigrant workers eked out a precarious living. Some had come from elsewhere in the Malayan archipelago, some from India or as far away as the Middle East, but the vast majority were from China. They had travelled to Singapore in order to escape the destitution and exploitation that was a staple of life in their homelands. They took whatever work they could get—labourers, noodle hawkers, rickshaw coolies—and they looked on Singapore as a temporary residence; their real allegiance was to the home town or village they had been forced to leave.

By 1900, ethnic Chinese had grown to account for nearly three quarters of the population, a ratio that is much the same today.

Yet geographically, Singapore sits at the heart of the Malay world. During the 20th century, residents of Singapore would have to weigh the issues of their fundamental loyalty—was it to China, Malaya, India, Britain or Singapore itself?

In the meantime, Singapore's openness to shipping, merchandise and people from all across the globe meant that it also took delivery of a different and invisible cargo—ideas. In the open culture of a port city, political ideologies from elsewhere circulated freely.

National Archives of Singapore

*Early Chinese immigrants
in Singapore*

*"Hardly anybody could remember a time when Victoria had not been
on the throne. And so it did symbolise the end of the age, and
particularly coming about the turn of the century as well."*
- Mary Turnbull, author, *"A History Of Singapore"*

David Ng, Courtesy of Natioanl Archives of Singapore

76

Sun Yat Sen visited Singapore regularly in the decade before the 1911 Revolution.

At the beginning of the 20th century one of the ascendant ideologies throughout the world revolved around national identity and national self-determination. This resonated with many in Singapore, where a growing sense of national awareness was given a cumulative boost by the 1911 Revolution in China that swept aside centuries of "alien" Manchu rule and launched an era in which rival politicians competed to show who was the most "patriotic". Significantly, the nominal leader of the Chinese revolution and the first President of the Republic of China (Taiwan), Sun Yat Sen, had visited Singapore regularly in the decade before the revolution. But this broad political awakening was remote from the sensibilities and interests of Singapore's Chinese elite. Known as the Straits Chinese, many of the most influential families had lived in the region for generations. They customarily spoke Malay rather than Chinese, and in many respects had a closer affinity to the British Empire than to the Chinese mainland.

"Sun Yat Sen was one of the first to articulate the idea that China should become a great power like England, France or America, Germany and so on, and that the way to do it was through nationalism."
- Wang Gung Wu, director, East Asian Institute

The Lee family of Kampung Java Road were typical Straits Chinese. They were intensely anglophile—giving their son an English first name, Harry, as well as a Chinese name. Though he would lead Singapore to independence, Lee Kuan Yew's upbringing was steeped in the colonial heritage that had developed and prospered among the Straits Chinese.

Sent to a Chinese school, Lee suffered for months because he did not understand the language and felt like an outsider. He persuaded his mother to transfer him to an English-language school. Here he encountered what he later described as a "remarkable imperial system", where even history and geography were taught not in general terms but in terms of the Empire.

"They were excited about the political future of China, so they started getting organised into groups, talked about politics, and here we see the start of a politicisation of the Chinese community in Singapore."
- Tan Tai Yong, dean, Faculty of Arts and Social Sciences, National University of Singapore

77

Lee Brothers Studio, Courtesy of National Archives of Singapore

Straits Chinese family, 1920s. Straits Chinese in Singapore were typically closer to the British and adopted Malay dress and customs, except during important Chinese festivals.

THE STRAITS CHINESE

Also known as Peranakans, the Straits Chinese are the descendants of Chinese immigrants who lived in the British Straits Settlements of Malaya and the Dutch-controlled islands of Java and Sumatra from as early as the 14th Century.

The Straits Chinese spoke Malay and absorbed Malay customs, especially those pertaining to food and dress, but retained some aspects of their Chinese heritage, including religion, nomenclature and ethnic identity. Intermarriage with the indigenous population was common.

In the 19th Century, many Straits Chinese were drawn to Singapore because of its commercial potential. With a long tradition of adapting to their surroundings, they embraced the conventions and customs of colonial society; they were educated at English-language schools and many held positions in the island's civil service.

This reinforced their identification with the British and led to the founding of the Straits Chinese British Association in 1900, which—as the "King's Chinese"—promised loyalty to Great Britain, and advanced the

The Peranakan Association, courtesy of National Archives of Singapore

Wedding of Wee Kim Tian and Teo Eng Kiat on 16th June 1936.

78

National Archives of Singapore

The Straits Chinese British Association's first committee.

welfare and higher education of citizens in the Straits Settlements. In turn, the British favoured the Straits Chinese for what was perceived as their neutral approach to ethnic identity.

One prominent Straits Chinese leader was Dr Lim Boon Keng (1869-1957). Lim was the first Chinese in Singapore to win the Queen's Scholarship, which allowed promising boys in the Straits Settlements to complete their studies in the United Kingdom. This enabled him to obtain a medical degree at the University of Edinburgh. He was a co-founder of OAC Insurance (the first locally owned insurance company to be established in Singapore); the United Saw Mills Limited of Singapore; the

Singapore Chinese Girls' School; the Chinese-language newspaper, *Thien Nan Shin Pao* and the English-language newspaper, *Malaya Tribune.*

Lim also served five terms on the Straits Settlements Legislative Council and had been appointed Justice of the Peace at the unprecedented age of 28. He was awarded the Order of

80

National Archives of Singapore

Dr Lim Boon Keng, circa 1890s. Lim was the first Chinese in Singapore to win the Queen's Scholarship.

the British Empire (OBE) in 1918, for his work and contributions to war charities. During the second Sino-Japanese war, Lim founded the Straits Chinese China Relief Fund Committee of Singapore, to support China's fight against the Japanese. When the Japanese occupied Singapore, Lim was persuaded by the Japanese to become the leader of the Overseas Chinese Association, a body meant to serve the needs of the local Chinese community under Japanese approval.

Straits Chinese leaders such as Lim were key members of Singapore's political elite in the colonial era. After the war—despite the fact that many of these English-educated Asians had turned against the British—power was transferred to them by the island's former colonial masters.

It should be noted that while "peranakan" means "local born" in Malay, it refers not only to the Peranakan or Straits Chinese, but also to similar communities in Southeast Asia with different ethnic origins, such as the Chitty Melaka (Indian), Kristang (Eurasian) and the Jawi Peranakans (Indian-Malay). Male descendants are referred to as Babas, while females are known as Nyonyas.

Most Peranakan Chinese are of Hokkien ancestry, and speak a dialect of the Malay language which contains many Hokkien words. However, both the Peranakan culture and language are slowly disappearing, as Singapore Peranakans, being ethnically Chinese, are assimilated into mainstream ethnic Chinese culture.

By the 1930s, British military power in the region was perilously outdated and overstretched. Official propaganda took pains to mask the Empire's vulnerability. In March 1938 the largest dry dock in the world—named after the new king, George VI—was opened in Singapore. It was the centrepiece of a naval base that had begun in 1923 and would not be completed until 1941. The base, together with Britain's other military assets in Singapore, was supposed to make the island impregnable. "It was imagined as a giant bastion, and the naval base itself was very impressive," Turnbull explained. "Ironically, though, it was bereft of ships. The army was only intended to hold the fort until the British Navy came to the rescue."

During the 1930s, life among the British in Singapore carried on as it had done for decades. Many did not see—or refused to acknowledge—portents of the coming conflagration. Japan's invasion of China in 1937 was widely viewed as a development that was politically as well as geographically remote from Singapore.

Reaction to the suffering of the mainland Chinese was understandably different among the inhabitants of Singapore's Chinatown. Nationalist feeling was fired by reports of atrocities in China, and Singapore experienced a wave of anti-Japanese sentiment.

82

Collection of KITLV, Liden, The Netherlands

ANTI-JAPANESE SENTIMENT

When Japan invaded China in 1937, overseas Chinese in particular those in Southeast Asia, looked for ways to help the motherland. United by hatred for the Japanese, the Chinese cultural elite in Singapore produced patriotic songs, dramas, comedies, films and commentaries that were disseminated through public broadcasts and performances in parks and streets.

Their fellow countrymen were in turn inspired and swept up in a wave of nationalistic fervour to give financial and moral support to China. These passionate anti-Japanese campaigns were accompanied by donations and fund-raising drives, of which flower-selling was the most common and the best supported. Drivers were also trained so that they could be sent to help in the effort to transport ammunition to Nationalist China from Southeast Asia.

Japanese canned food, cotton and rubber products were all popular at this time because they were cheaper than products made in the West. However, anti-Japanese feeling was such that anyone who bought or sold Japanese goods risked attack.

Chinese merchants who did not take part in the boycott of Japanese goods were first warned by members of the National Vanguard Corps (NVC), which was formed by activists to retaliate against the Japanese. If they resisted, these traders would find their shops and signboards daubed with black paint by NVC members. The aim was to shame such "traitors". If this failed, the merchants would be subject to serious physical violence, and in some cases shopkeepers had their ears cut off for continuing to sell Japanese goods.

" 'To cut off an ear' was the most severe punishment meted out to merchants who openly supported Japanese aggressors," NVC member Choo Kim Seng said in an interview in the book "Eternal Vigilance: The Price of Freedom", published in 1999. "We worked within guide-lines. We would not hurt any other part of the traitor's body. ... This was an effective deterrent, and we only targeted unscrupulous merchants of Chinese origin. People hated

83

Chinese theatre in Singapore, 1920.

❧

"The fury among the Chinese in Singapore galvanised them into action. Not only did they organise themselves to raise funds to support the fight against Japan and sing songs of protest, they tried to hit Japan where it hurts—by boycotting the cheap Japanese goods that were coming into Singapore at that time."
– Tan Tai Yong, dean, Faculty of Arts and Social Sciences,
National University of Singapore

❧

84

Photo by Keystone, Getty Images

Chinese Refugees enter the French Concession in Nantao during the second Sino-Japanese war, 1937

unscrupulous and pro-Japanese Chinese merchants, so although cutting off ears was a crime, nobody ever reported these cases to the police."

Tan Kah Kee, Singapore's "Rubber King" who had made his fortune from plantations in Malaya and factories in Singapore, was the de facto leader of the Chinese community in Singapore going into the war. Tan played a key role in mobilising support for the Chinese in the second Sino-Japanese War. In Singapore, he organised various agencies, including the China Relief Fund Federation in Southeast Asia.

Tan said later the China Relief Fund raised the equivalent of $140 million in 1939 and 1940. Such efforts were tolerated in the Straits Settlements on the condition that the money be used to offer relief to refugees and wounded soldiers, but not to support the war directly. The caveat was made to avoid antagonising Japan. But the funds raised were delivered to the Executive Yuan, the executive branch of the Republic of China, and were likely used for any purpose it deemed appropriate.

85

WAR ERUPTS

Those involved in anti-Japanese activities felt safe, protected by Britain's military might and confident that the Japanese would never be able to reach them. In this they were mistaken, and in the coming years some would pay dearly for this mistake.

On a quiet Sunday morning in December 1941, Japanese planes attacked Pearl Harbour. Just hours later, Japan's strike southward into Southeast Asia began.

War had come to the region, and Singapore would be one of its most spectacular victims.

Chapter 5

THE WAR AND AFTERWARDS

War came quickly to Singapore, with the first Japanese air raid just three hours after the surprise attack on Pearl Harbour. Japanese troops had already landed in northern Malaya.

"Singapore's first blitz came just a few hours after the opening of hostilities from Japanese planes from off an aircraft carrier," a British newsreel of the time reported. "A number of bombs falling in a Chinese district of the city caused much damage and heavy casualties among the civil population. The centre of the city, where the big European shops and hotels are situated didn't escape. Bombs fell on Raffles Square and other spots equally well-known to every Far East tourist and traveller."

Lee Kuan Yew, the country's future prime minister, was in his dormitory when the bombs started falling just after 4 am. Another eyewitness, Othman Wok, recalled the initial excitement he felt, which was followed by grim reality.

"The siren sounded. I ran to the field," said Wok, who later served as Lee's minister of social affairs. "I wanted to see an airplane—very excited about it; it was the first time. I could hear the sounds of the engine.

"It was only when the all-clear siren sounded that the extent of the damage and horrors of war hit home. Houses crumbled from the bombing, the dead lay in the streets, and the paramedics tried to help those who were injured and take them to hospital. In the gruesome setting, people ran around helplessly, gripped by fear and panic."

National Archives of Singapore

A Japanese propaganda poster, circa 1940.

Preceding Page: Indian workers clearing rubble following a Japanese air raid on Singapore.

Getty Images

Women and children being herded together by Japanese soldiers after the fall of Singapore, February 1942.

The initial raid was followed by another the next day, and still more over the course of the week. Hundreds died, and many more were injured. Singapore began to look like a "fortress", *Life* magazine reported. Japanese on the island were unwelcome.

89

"The Japanese are promptly rounded up in Singapore and taken away for internment," the British newsreel reported, stretching into hyperbole. "The Japanese who had carried out many trades and professions in Malaya had one favourite trade: that of spying."

Meanwhile, Japanese troops that had landed 500 miles to the north in Malaya were quickly advancing southward. Light tanks and infantrymen in bicycles surprised the British defenders with the speed of their advance along jungle paths that connected rubber plantations. The Japanese had already neutralized the Royal Air Force in the region, and torpedo bombers sank

"Houses crumbled from the bombing, the dead lay on the streets, and paramedics tried to help those who were injured and take them to hospital. In this gruesome setting, people ran around helplessly, gripped by fear and panic"

— Othman Wok, minister of foreign affairs, 1963-1977

two warships—the battleship *HMS Prince of Wales* and the battle cruiser *HMS Repulse*—as they raced up the Malaya coast.

Arms were issued to the Malay, Chinese and Indian communities. Weeks before, these men had been labourers, hawkers and rickshaw coolies. Now they stood as equals with their colonial masters, the British.

As Singapore braced itself for the Japanese onslaught, this motley crew of armed men prepared to die in defence of an island that few, until then, had truly considered home.

On 8 February 1942, just two months after they had landed in northern Malaya and following a lightning advance, Japanese troops crossed the narrow straits and established a beachhead on the island of Singapore.

The 30,000 strong Japanese assault force faced more than twice as many defenders under British command, but the Japanese had control of the air, and they had the massive psychological advantage of being at the end of a campaign in which they had systematically outfought the Empire forces opposing them. The battle for Singapore lasted just one week. On 15 February the British surrendered to the Japanese at a ceremony in the Ford Motor Factory at Bukit Timah.

British Prime Minister Winston Churchill described the fall of Singapore as the "worst disaster and largest capitulation in British history".

More than a century after Raffles first raised the Union Jack over the island, British commanders arrived to meet their Japanese counterparts under a white flag.

The Japanese forces advanced towards Singapore, 1942.

WHY THE BRITISH LOST TO THE JAPANESE

How did Singapore, which had been thought by many to be impregnable, fall so quickly and easily to the Japanese?

To begin with there had been a complacent and counterproductive underestimation of the prowess and resourcefulness of Japanese troops. In addition, once the Japanese had landed in Malaya, they consistently wrong-footed British political and military leaders, who failed to regain the initiative throughout the two-month campaign.

Many of the Allied field commanders were inexperienced, and the troops under British command were drawn from disparate military and cultural traditions. In addition to units raised locally there were British, Australian, New Zealand, Indian and Nepalese Gurkha contingents in the army defending Singapore. These troops were never brought together into a single cohesive fighting force; defenders were disorganised, poorly trained and, as the tide of battle continued to favour the Japanese, morale was chronically low.

Communications were severely hampered by Japanese air superiority, and following the sinking by Japanese planes on 10 December 1941 of the British battleship, *HMS Prince of Wales*, and the battlecruiser, *HMS Repulse*, the British defenders of Singapore had no effective Royal Navy support.

Japanese infantry and a tankette on the Causeway in Singapore, 1942. Less than two meters wide, these light tanks surprised British commanders with their ability to race through the Malay jungles.

National Archives of Singapore

British Prime Minister Winston Churchill described the fall of Singapore as the "worst disaster and largest capitulation in British history".

92

"The Tiger of Malaya," Japanese Gen. Tomoyuki Yamashita led his troops to victory in Malaya and Singapore.

Associated Press

Finally, when he made the decision to surrender on 15 February, the British Commander, Lieutenant-General Arthur Percival, had been told that ammunition and water supplies on the island were sufficient to last only until the following day. What he did not know was that his Japanese counterpart, Lieutenant-General Tomoyuki Yamashita, had been told that his troops had exhausted their own ammunition reserves and would be unable to renew their attack if the British did not surrender.

Historian W. David McIntyre with the University of Canterbury in New Zealand said the lack of air support was a critical factor in the fall of Singapore, but also noted that Singapore's defences were pointed toward the sea and badly equipped for an attack from Malaya.

"The initial preparations were against a naval attack, so they put 1914-18 war guns set in turrets around the island," McIntyre explained. "It is true that some of these were on all-round swivels so in theory they could be used against a land attack, but they had armour-piercing shells that would only have made holes in the ground."

Famously, the Japanese employed a fleet of bicycles to hasten their advance down the Malayan Peninsula. The flexibility that Japanese commanders showed, tactically and logistically, was in sharp contrast to the ponderous performance of the British colonial troops who opposed them.

93

"From City Hall, the prisoners of war were forced to walk to Changi Prison. The Japanese told us village folk to stand by the roadside in order to shame the white men who had once been the big masters, the managers, bosses, important people. Now they had become the small people, lowly. The white men had fallen, the Japanese had risen."
– Mohammad Anis bin Tairan, witness

*After the surrender, the Japanese lost no time in publicly
humiliating the island's former masters. Singapore was renamed
Syonan (or Syonanto), meaning "Light of the South".*

Japanese soldiers travelled light, carrying as few rations as possible, and living off the land or from supplies left by the retreating British. They made optimal use of speed and surprise and displayed a ruthless determination and confidence that was largely absent among the troops facing them. The Japanese invaders were also under strict orders to take no prisoners since handling captives would slow down the offensive.

After the surrender, the Japanese lost no time in publicly humiliating the island's former masters.

Singapore was renamed *Syonan-to*, meaning "Light of the South". As the island's new masters, the Japanese proclaimed a common Asian brotherhood. This appeal to Asian solidarity was designed to win support for Japan's war aims among the local population, particularly among the Malays and Indians.

94

National Archives of Singapore

*Prisoners of war at the Sime Road camp in Japanese-occupied
Syonan-to, the name the Japanese gave Singapore, 1942.*

SOOK CHING

The Chinese were singled out for retribution because of their vocal opposition in previous years to the Japanese invasion of the Chinese mainland. The cruel treatment of Singapore's Chinese population during the Japanese Occupation was to change the course of the island's history.

Immediately after the British surrender, the new Japanese authorities began a process of purging, or *Sook Ching.* Over a period of just under three weeks, Chinese males from every walk of life were interrogated at screening centres across the island.

95

Popper Foto/Getty Images

Some of the 120,000 British, Australian, Indian and Chinese forces captured by the Japanese forces.

"Then, after the commotion of the trucks, there was suddenly silence. The silence was followed by the sound of gunfire. I heard screaming and loud orders in Japanese for the shooters to hurry up. It was all noisy for a short space of time. Then silence."
— Mohammad Anis bin Tairan, witness

96

Most Singaporeans had no idea of what to expect when they were told to report to screening centres. Japanese police raided Chinese homes, ordered residents to report for screening and searched for fugitives and for evidence of involvement in pre-war anti-Japanese activities and hidden arms.

Notices and posters were put up. Through loud-speakers, the Chinese population was informed that men between the ages of 18 and 50 were to report to various centres for screening. Sometimes, news came by word of mouth from neighbours or friends.

Screeners were supposedly looking for volunteers, communists and criminals. But the screening process was arbitrary. People's lives depended on the whim of Japanese soldiers.

At one centre, men with glasses were judged to be educated and thus by implication guilty of anti-Japanese activities. At another, businessmen, civil servants and students were singled out. Soft hands were taken as evidence that an individual was educated and was likely to have pro-British sympathies. The Japanese also made use of hooded informers, who identified candidates for execution simply with a nod of the head.

Nineteen-year-old Harry Lee Kuan Yew was among a group of men rounded up for interrogation by the Japanese.

"They asked me to leave the pack, to join a certain group where other young men were going," Lee recounted years later. "I felt unease. I said, 'Oh this is bad,' because I was a tall, lanky youth. I said, 'Oh, they must think that I'm a soldier,' and I wasn't. So I said, 'Would you mind if I go collect my things?' So they said, 'Yes, go ahead.' So I ran back and laid low."

The number of Chinese civilians murdered by Japanese troops in the three weeks after the British surrender is generally estimated to be between 25,000 and 50,000.

Others were far less fortunate. The Japanese claimed after the war that only a few thousand were killed during the massacre in Singapore, but witnesses and other observers put the figure at closer to 50,000. *Sook Ching* victims were forced into lorries. Often they were interrogated or tortured before being taking to killing grounds in remote areas such as Punggol, Changi and Bedok. There they were machine-gunned or bayoneted. Mass graves were found in these areas after the war.

Mohammed Anis bin Tairan, a witness to the atrocities, told Discovery Channel, "From the back of my house I could hear the noise from the trucks, making me think, 'Is there more fighting breaking out?' Then, after the commotion of the trucks, there was suddenly silence. The silence was followed by the sound of gunfire. I heard screaming and loud orders in Japanese for the shooters to hurry up. It was all noisy for a short space of time. Then silence."

Many, like Lee, were able to avoid capture by laying low in their native Singapore. Others were able to flee the island entirely. Tan Kah Kee, the "Rubber King" and driving force behind the China Relief Fund, found refuge in Java, Indonesia. Not finding Tan in Singapore, the Japanese nonetheless issued false reports that he had been captured. Tan's motorcycle repairman was located, however, and in a show of brutality was tied behind a motorcycle and dragged through the streets.

97

"They asked me to leave the pack, to join a certain group where other young men were going. I felt unease, I said, 'Oh, this is bad,"
– Lee Kuan Yew, first prime minister of Singapore

THE OCCUPATION

The ferocity of *Sook Ching* lasted for about three weeks following the fall of Singapore. In March and April, the occupying forces tried to create civil administration of the island. While the military administration would maintain overall control, the civil apparatus would oversee mundane functions through communal and neighbourhood organizations. In the background, however, the feared military police, the *Kempeitai*, remained active and continued their brutal tactics against any hint of anti-Japanese activities.

The Japanese invaders stressed their vision of creating an Asian brotherhood, which necessitated driving the white man out. They needed local populations to accept their fate, in large part because combat troops were needed on the front lines, and Japanese authorities didn't want soldiers tied up keeping the peace in occupied territories.

"Day-to-day life had to go on under the Japanese occupation," Lee wrote in his memoirs. "At first everyone felt lost. ... We felt danger all around us. Knowing somebody in authority, whether a Japanese or Taiwanese interpreter with links to the Japanese, was very important and could be a life saver."

Lee busied himself studying Mandarin (he had been educated in English) and Japanese, which he found easier. For little more than a year, he worked as a clerk for various businesses, and then in 1943 he secured a job as an English editor for *Hodobu*, the Japanese information or propaganda department. "My job was to run through cables of allied news agencies," Lee wrote. "Radio signals were not clear in the late afternoons and early evenings, and because reception was poor, many, many words were garbled or lost. My job was to decipher them and fill in the missing bits, guided by context, as in a word puzzle."

RATIONING

During the Japanese Occupation, normal trade through Singapore's bustling port came to a halt. Rationing was eventually applied to almost all goods, with the list of controlled items growing by the day. Residents had to register for a ration card, which contained details of the holder's gender and age, with the amount of rations differing between men, women and children.

People had to queue for hours, sometimes in the middle of the night, to buy scarce provisions. Rations were given out in weekly portions, or simply when they were available, which meant that people spent much of their lives standing in queues.

A copy of a registration card issued by the Food Control Department of the Rationing Office during the Japanese Occupation, 1942.

National Archives of Singapore

Prices were controlled, but the quality of goods was poor. As rice stocks became harder and harder to come by, people turned to substitutes that were relatively easy to grow, such as tapioca and sweet potatoes. Those who had a bit of land also grew vegetables for their own consumption.

The situation worsened as the occupation continued, with people living in constant need and under a growing sense of vulnerability. Many adopted desperate remedies, and resorted to theft, a crime that, if characterised as "looting", could result in execution.

It didn't take long for a black market in essential supplies to develop. Some of these controlled items came from the Japanese themselves, as members of the occupation force sought to profit from shortages. Not only did the black market serve to encourage corruption, it also caused uncontrollable and widespread inflation. Amid hardship and chaos, malnutrition was endemic, and many died of hunger.

100

Japanese-issued paper currency, nick-named "banana notes" because of the pictures of banana trees and other tropical fruit printed on the bills, compounded the economic chaos on the island. The Japanese notes had no serial numbers and were printed on poor quality paper. When more money was needed, the Occupation authorities simply printed more notes, fuelling an inflationary spiral. As economic conditions worsened and the currency continued to depreciate, notes were issued in ever larger denominations until the currency was so devalued that "banana money" became synonymous with worthless paper.

National Archives of Singapore

Japanese currency notes of $0.50 & $1.00.

THE KEMPEITAI

The *Kempeitai* was the military police force deployed by the Japanese War Ministry in the occupied territories. Originally formed in 1881, it developed into an organisation that focused on destroying resistance to Japanese military rule. The *Kempeitai* was universally feared; its officers had authority to arrest at will, and they were trained in brutal methods of interrogation.

During the Japanese Occupation of Singapore, the strength of the 200 regular *Kempeitai* officers was bolstered by another 1,000 supplementary officers drafted from the army. Prisoners of war came under the supervision of the *Kempeitai*, who were notorious for their savagery. The *Sook Ching* Massacre was the work of the 2nd Field *Kempeitai*, which had accompanied the 25th Army during the Malaya Campaign.

The *Kempeitai* maintained offices and torture chambers in various locations, including the YMCA building on Stamford Road, the Central Police Station on South Bridge Road, a private home in Smith Street and a garage on Oxley Road. The YMCA Building was a notorious house of horrors—victims were seen being dragged in for interrogation, and screams could be heard from the building by passers-by. The old Art Deco building has since been demolished.

101

The Kempeitai *was universally feared; its officers had authority to arrest at will, and they were trained in brutal methods of interrogation.*

INTERROGATION METHODS

The Japanese military police, the dreaded *Kempeitai* officers, were not only empowered to arrest anyone, but also had absolute discretion to do whatever they liked, acting as police, investigator, judge, jury and executioner. Little evidence, if any, was required to take victims into custody. Rounding up suspects, the *Kempeitai* made use of spies from the local community; informers were not required to prove their allegations, which meant that many were falsely accused out of jealousy, or taken into custody because of rumour or a careless remark. The result was a climate of fear and suspicion. After they were arrested, victims had no recourse; even if released, they always faced the possibility of being arrested again.

Customarily, suspects were arrested in the middle of the night, and held in filthy conditions, men and women together, until taken for interrogation. Some victims were tortured to death.

One of the *Kempetai*'s preferred methods of torture involved forcing a hose down the victim's throat and filling the stomach with water, which was then forced out of the body by beatings or by one of the interrogators jumping on the victim's stomach. Alternatively, the victim's head would be immersed in a tub of water until just before drowning. Another torture technique involved forcing large quantities of uncooked rice down the prisoner's throat and then pumping in water to expand the rice. Severe beatings were common, and interrogators also inflicted pain through electric shocks and burning. In addition, prisoners were subjected to the systematic breaking and dislocation of limbs through quasi-surgical torture techniques; using pliers to remove fingernails was a common practice.

Physical torture was compounded by psychological cruelty—prisoners would be told they were to be executed and guards would go through the motions of preparing for the execution, right up to the final moment and then the prisoner would be taken back to his cell. In other cases, prisoners were forced to watch while members of their families were tortured.

THE JAPANESE SURRENDER

The end of World War II began with the Allies dropping an atomic bomb on Hiroshima in Japan on 6 August 1945. The blast killed 140,000 people. After a second atomic bomb was dropped on Nagasaki, on 9 August, killing 80,000, Emperor Hirohito instructed his government to accept the surrender terms laid out in the Potsdam Declaration issued by the United States, Britain and China on 26 July 1945. On 15 August 1945, Japan formally and unconditionally surrendered to the Allies.

In Singapore, news of the surrender filtered down to the population, though there were fears that some local Japanese commanders would fight on regardless of orders from Tokyo. The Japanese garrison on the island was believed to have enough ammunition and supplies of food to last more than a year. Although this did not happen, a large number of Japanese officers on the island committed suicide rather than face the humiliation of being taken prisoner.

103

"The Tiger of Malaya", Tomoyuki Yamashita, in prison in Manila after signing the surrender documents. He was hanged in Manila for war crimes.

Getty Images

"Well I was here that afternoon in 1945, with hundreds of people. When they saw the generals marching past with the guards looking downcast, they shouted at them 'bagero[1], bagero'. 'Bagero' means 'bloody fool' in the Japanese language. Everybody joined in, huge crowd, they say, 'bagero, bagero, bagero', many, many times, until they went into the room."

- Othman Wok, minister of social affairs, 1963-1977

104

While waiting for the British to arrive, the Japanese prepared their own internment camp in Jurong. "Banana notes" were now completely worthless, and during the 19-day interregnum between the end of Japanese authority and the arrival of the British, the island descended into economic and civil chaos. Some of those who had collaborated with the Japanese managed to slip away, but others were hunted down and murdered, accused of being traitors and informers. Anarchy reigned and there was rampant looting.

British warships finally arrived at the Tanjong Pagar docks on September 5 and the Commonwealth troops were met with spontaneous cheering. On September 12, the surrender ceremony was held at the Municipal Building (now City Hall). Eleven copies of the Instrument of Surrender were signed by General Seishiro Itagaki, on behalf of Hisaichi Terauchi, Supreme Commander of Imperial Japanese Forces, Southern Region. Terauchi had suffered a stroke at the beginning of May and was physically unable to attend the surrender ceremony. The surrender was taken by Admiral Lord Louis Mountbatten, Supreme Allied Commander, Southeast Asia.

Collection of the KITLV, Leiden, The Netherlands

The Japanese delegates leaving Singapore's town hall after signing the surrender documents, 1945.

---

[1] Local usage for the Japanese expression "baka yaru".

The ceremony ended with the raising of the Union Jack—the same one that had been carried during the British surrender in 1942, and which had been kept hidden in Changi Prison. But although there was an outpouring of relief in Singapore that the brutal Japanese occupation had been brought to an end, and although the British were welcomed back as liberators, the myth of British invincibility had been exposed, and Britain would never again command the kind of authority, in Singapore or in other parts of Asia, that it had once enjoyed. Having failed to defend Singapore, it could no longer claim to a natural right to govern the island.

In 1947, seven Japanese army and police officers were tried for the *Sook Ching* atrocities. Two were sentenced to death. The others were sentenced to life imprisonment. All except one were repatriated to Japan when the American Occupation of Japan ended in 1952.

The Japanese government subsequently exonerated the convicted men. Colonel Masanobu Tsuji, the officer widely acknowledged in Japanese military circles to have had overall responsibility for the *Sook Ching* massacres, was in charge of supervising the screening process. Never brought to justice, he went into hiding at the end of the war and resurfaced in Japan in 1948. He became a member of parliament and an author before mysteriously disappearing in 1961.

105

Singapore Tourism Board, courtesy of National Archives of Singapore

Lord Mountbatten addresses the people of Singapore after accepting the Japanese surrender.

Singaporeans took note that few of the Japanese responsible for atrocities during the occupation of Singapore were punished, but rather simply deported by the British. This was regarded as an outrage by the Chinese community. Many began to argue that the spilling of so much Chinese blood on Singapore soil justified a moral claim to govern the island that had not existed before the war.

Lee said later, "It was the catastrophic consequences of the war that changed mindsets, that my generation decided, 'No, this doesn't make sense. We should be able to run this as well as the British did, if not better'."

Meanwhile, Britain—exhausted and practically bankrupted by the war—had lost its appetite for empire. In the upper echelons of the Colonial Office a radical plan for the region was being drawn up.

For more than a hundred years, the British administration of Singapore had been closely entwined with that of neighbouring Malaya. But now, the futures of the two territories would diverge. The British

106

Parliament decided that while Malaya would be groomed for independence, Singapore was to remain a crown colony, at least provisionally. The relationship between Singapore and Malaya would come to dominate the politics of both countries. In the post-war years, however, events in China had a more direct impact on the region, with the communist victory in China in 1949 sending shockwaves throughout Asia.

Workers after the war clean remains of victims of Sook Ching. The remains of an estimated 2,000 victims were found in this one mass grave.

Associated Press

MEMORIAL

The Civilian War Memorial at Beach Road, unveiled in 1967 by then Prime Minister Lee Kuan Yew, was built to commemorate civilians who lost their lives during the Japanese Occupation. The remains of unidentified war victims are buried beneath it. Some managed to survive the screening and joined bands of guerrillas fighting the Japanese in the jungle.

Lee Kuan Yew recalled that the Japanese Occupation had imparted a bitter lesson on the nature of power: "That if you controlled a country by force, and the lives of the people depended upon you, you can make them comply, you can even change their attitudes to you, at least openly, make them comply."

107

Singapore Tourism Board

War Memorial

LEFTISTS GAIN GROUND

During the war, Chinese guerrillas had fought the Japanese in the jungles of Malaya. In the late 1940s and early 1950s they turned their attention to the British. The result was a costly, low-intensity war. It did not take long before communist agitation spilled over into Singapore itself.

For a decade the global ideological clash between communism and capitalism was played out in Singapore.

Political discord was fomented in many of the island's schools. During the turbulent 1950s, the Chinese education system operated beyond the effective supervision of the colonial authorities. And from the Chinese High School came young idealists, imbued with the teachings of Chairman Mao Tse-Tung and other left-wing thinkers.

Two young men, in particular, stood out. They were Lim Chin Siong and Fong Swee Suan. Fong later recalled for Discovery Channel, "In my Chinese High School class was a boy named Lim Chin Siong. I was very impressed when I first met him because he was very courteous and truly sincere. China's recent successes left a very deep impact on us. Both of us were strongly against colonialism."

In a regional climate where non-communist countries experienced rapid growth and communist regimes were obliged to introduce market mechanisms, the attractiveness of communist ideology went into steep decline.

LEFTIST ORGANISERS

In the aftermath of the Japanese occupation, political energy swept through Singapore. As many began to question the legitimacy of British rule, some began exploring other political models. Two that would eventually stand out as key players in Singapore's journey to independence would be Lim Chin Siong and his political lieutenant Fong Swee Suan. Both would be dogged by accusations of being communists and would eventually be jailed as Lee Kuan Yew solidified his hold on power.

Lim was born in Singapore in 1933, but his family moved to Johor in Malaya during the Great Depression. He returned to Singapore after the Japanese surrender, where he resumed his studies at Catholic High School before transferring to Chinese High School in 1950. Born in 1931, Fong became fast friends with Lim when he, too, transferred to Chinese High School.

They organised a boycott of exams in 1951 as part of the Singapore Students' Anti-British League. Lim was later questioned by the Special Police and expelled from school, but Fong managed to avoid being caught.

By the mid-1950s, Lim and Fong became Singapore's most powerful union leaders. In his memoirs, Lee Kuan Yew wrote of first meeting the pair in 1954. "They were soft spoken and could understand a little English, but had brought (an interpreter)," he wrote, adding he was "excited" to be exploring the Chinese-educated working class as recruits to his cause. "Lim and Fong looked the right type: well-mannered, earnest and sincere in demeanour, simple on their clothes. Keenness and dedication were written in every line of their faces and in every gesture."

The three became political allies, but the allegiance would shatter before Singapore found its independence.

109

THE MALAYAN COMMUNIST PARTY

In the decade after World War II, communist regimes were established in China, North Korea and North Vietnam and communist movements exerted major political influence throughout East Asia. There were communist-led insurgencies in Burma, Thailand, Indonesia and the Philippines.

The Malayan Communist Party (MCP) founded in 1930 was the dominant force behind armed resistance to the Japanese occupation of Malaya and Singapore. It established the Malayan People's Anti-Japanese Army (MPAJA) in March 1942. Officers who went on to lead the MPAJA received military training from the British immediately before the fall of Singapore in February 1942. Later, the Royal Air Force dropped arms and other supplies to the MPAJA.

After the war the MCP campaigned for an end to British colonial rule. The organisation developed extensive grassroots support, particularly through its influence in trade unions and student unions. In the summer of 1948, unions which the British claimed were communist controlled were proscribed, and the MCP was made illegal.

This was followed by 12 years of low-intensity warfare between the British forces and the Malayan National Liberation Army (MNLA), the new incarnation of the MPAJA. The conflict became know as The Emergency.

In Singapore the MCP's military campaign focused on assassination and intimidation accompanied by strikes. The authorities responded by arresting key MCP leaders and breaking up the network of party cells on the island.

The independence of Malaysia in 1957 took away the MNLA's call for liberation, and a military defeat in 1958 sapped the army of most of its remaining strength. The government declared the Emergency over in 1960. By then, only a small number of guerrillas remained active and they were largely confined to a narrow belt of territory straddling the Thai border.

Throughout the 1970s and '80s, the Singapore authorities argued that potential communist agitation continued to represent a threat to national security. However, with serious penalties imposed on those accused of being communist or pro-communist, any real communist influence on day-to-day politics was negligible. In a regional climate where non-communist countries experienced rapid growth and communist regimes were obliged to introduce market mechanisms, the attractiveness of communist ideology went into steep decline.

On 2 December 1989, following years of military inactivity, the MCP formally signed peace agreements with the Malaysian and Thai governments ending its armed struggle.

111

Collection of the KITLV, Leiden, The Netherlands

Allied ships dot Singapore harbour following the surrender of the Japanese. This view is from the Cathay, at the time one of Singapore's most modern buildings and erstwhile headquarters for the occupying Japanese.

Chapter 6

THE LEADER
AND HIS PARTY

By the 1950s, the British were committed to introducing democracy in Singapore, and the governor announced plans for the island's first general elections, giving citizens the chance to participate in the political process, and creating opportunities for those who were familiar with the British system of government and administration, such as Harry Lee.

Lee's educational background was a world apart from the students who attended Chinese High School. He had spent four years studying law in London. While he was there he participated in discussions with other students about the future of Singapore.

After graduation, Lee returned home, his interest in politics burgeoning.

114

National Archives of Singapore

1957: People's Action Party (PAP) leader Lee Kuan Yew re-elected in a by-election to represent Tanjong Pagar in the Legislative Assembly.

Preceding page: In 1959 the prime minister, Mr Lee Kuan Yew, said that the people of Singapore would begin to see "the fruits of the PAP Government's Five Year Plan" as early as 1961. There would be more factories and more jobs for the people of the island, he declared.

LEE KUAN YEW

16 September 1923	Harry Lee Kuan Yew is born in Singapore.
1936-39, 1940-42	Studies at Raffles Institution and Raffles College.
15 February 1942	Singapore captured and occupied by the Japanese.
September 1945	British return to Singapore.
1946-50	Studies at Cambridge and London.
December 1947	Secretly marries Kwa Geok Choo in Britain.
June 1948	State of Emergency declared in Malaya and Singapore.
August 1950	Returns to Singapore.
September 1950	Marries Kwa again in Singapore.
1952	Birth of first child, son Hsien Loong.
1950-59	Practises law, active as legal adviser to several trade unions.
November 1954	Founding of People's Action Party (PAP).
1955	Birth of second child, daughter Wei Ling.

115

April 1955	Elected to the Legislative Assembly under new Rendel Constitution. PAP wins three seats. Lee becomes leader of the opposition.
October 1956	Arrest and detention of left-wing United Front leaders.
1957	Birth of third child, son Hsien Yang.
31 August 1957	Federation of Malaya becomes independent.
December 1957	PAP wins 13 seats in City Council election.
30 May 1959	PAP wins 43 out of 51 seats in general election under the new constitution.

116

Singapore Press Holdings

Swearing-in ceremony of the Singapore cabinet at the City Council Hall 5 June 1959.

4 June 1959	United Front leaders released from detention.
5 June 1959	Sworn in as prime minister of the self-governing state of Singapore at age 35.
February 1960	Establishes Housing and Development Board with Lim Kim San as chairman. Begins massive public housing programme.
July 1960	Forms People's Association to mobilise grassroots support to counter communists.
August 1961	Thirteen left-wing PAP assemblymen break away to form Barisan Sosialis.
September 1961	Lee gives series of radio talks designed to expose communist conspiracy and urges support for merger with Malaya.

Singapore Press Holdings

A ceremony on City Hall steps in Singapore marking the island-state's Union with Malaya to form Malaysia independent of British rule, 16 September 1963.

September 1962	Singaporeans vote for merger with Malaya in a referendum.
February 1963	Operation Coldstore detains left-wing activists and their supporters.
31 August 1963	Singapore declares independence, ahead of formation of Malaysia.
16 September 1963	Malaysia formed, comprising Malaya, Singapore, Sarawak and Sabah.
21 September 1963	PAP wins general election in Singapore.
March 1964	Difficulties with federal government increase.
April 1964	The Port of Singapore Authority (PSA) established as a statutory board.
21 July 1964	Communal riots in Singapore on Prophet Mohammed's Birthday.
September 1964	Second outbreak of communal violence.
January–February 1965	Unsuccessful discussions between Lee and the Tunku Abdul Rahman regarding "rearrangements" within Malaysia.
July 1965	The Tunku decides Singapore must leave Malaysia.
9 August 1965	Singapore's separation from Malaysia.

Ministry of Information and the Arts, courtesy of National Archives of Singapore

National Service Registration, 1967.

September 1965	Five-year Mass Family Planning programme introduced to reduce birth rate.
Early 1967	Lee first moots idea of transforming Singapore into a tropical garden city
March 1967	National Service Bill for all male citizens passed.
April 1968	General election boycotted by Barisan Socialis. Seven contested seats won by PAP with 84 per cent of votes cast.
August 1968	Employment Act and Industrial Relations (Amendment) Act introduced.

May 1969	Race riot in Singapore following bloody race riots in Kuala Lumpur after Malaysian general election.
September 1972	General election. PAP wins all contested seats, with 69 per cent of votes cast.
1972	Two-child family policy promoted.
December 1976	General election. PAP wins all contested seats, with 72 per cent of votes cast. Goh Chok Tong enters parliament.
December 1980	General election. PAP wins all contested seats with 78 per cent of votes cast.
October 1981	JB Jeyaretnam, secretary general of Workers' Party, wins by-election, breaking PAP's 13-year monopoly in parliament.
1983	Lee raises issue of unmarried graduate women. Encourages educated women to marry and have more children.
December 1984	General elections. PAP loses seat to Chiam See Tong, then-secretary-general of the Singapore Democratic Party. Jeyaretnam retains his seat with an increased majority. PAP's share of the vote declines to 64 per cent. Some attribute PAP's reduced majority to Lee's unpopular Graduate Mother Scheme offering incentives to graduate women to marry and have children.

Hsien Loong, Lee's elder son, enters parliament at age 32. |

Singapore Prime Minister Goh Chok Tong, right and Senior Minister Lee Kuan Yew, 2001.

AFP

January 1985	New cabinet. Lee withdraws from daily administration, but remains a dominant influence.
1987	Deputy Prime Minister Goh Chok Tong announces end of two-child policy. Incentives to encourage return to three-or four-child families.
May 1987	Internal Security Act invoked to arrest a group of alleged Marxist conspirators.
September 1988	General election. Last election with Lee as prime minister.
	PAP wins election, with 63 per cent of the vote. Chiam retains his seat. Jeyaretnam is prevented from standing because of court ruling against him.
	Lee the last remaining member of PAP old guard in parliament.

November 1990	Lee steps down as prime minister in favour of Goh.
	Goh appoints Lee to cabinet position of senior minister and Lee Hsien Loong as one of two deputy prime ministers.
August 1991	General election. Goh's first election as prime minister. PAP wins with 61 per cent of the vote, losing four seats to the opposition.
November 1992	Lee resigns as secretary general of PAP.
January 1997	General election. PAP wins with 64 per cent of the vote, recapturing two of the four seats lost in 1991.
August 2004	Lee Hsien Loong succeeds Goh as prime minister. Lee appointed to new cabinet position of minister mentor, while Goh is given the position of senior minister.

Along with a group of friends who had been with him in London, Lee embarked on the process of building a political party. He and his colleagues had to learn from scratch how to establish an organisational structure and then attract popular support.

Then as now, any political party that aspired to govern Singapore had to win the support of the Chinese-speaking majority. Rather than adopting a nationalist stance, the PAP focused on bread-and-butter issues that had resonance with the Chinese and other communities. The party drew up a programme of initiatives aimed at raising living standards, building more public housing and creating jobs.

Throughout the 1950s Singaporeans had looked to the trade unions to advance their interests in these areas, not to the graduates of British universities.

From the trade unions came two of the most influential political figures of the late 1950s and early 1960s—Lim Chin Siong and his school friend, Fong Swee Suan.

The support of trade union leaders was critical for anyone aspiring to political office.

123

Harry Lee had already made a key symbolic gesture by adopting his Chinese name in public—Lee Kuan Yew. Now, he began a series of meetings with Lim, Fong and other union leaders.

Together, they formed a new political party, the People's Action Party (PAP). The party was launched in November 1954 in the same building where the film of Queen Victoria's funeral had been shown just over half a century earlier.

Tan Tai Yong, dean of the National University of Singapore's Faculty of Arts and Social Sciences, said the joining of the unionists and Lee's moderates was a

"We were very disciplined and were willing to make sacrifices. The advantage of a Chinese education is that we were full of ideals and were determined to reform society."
– Fong Swee Suan, secretary general, Singapore Bus Workers' Union

"In a way it (the PAP) was a coming together of two disparate groups of people: an English-educated group of moderates, and a Chinese-educated group of militants, both having the same objectives, of wanting to achieve self-government and eventual political independence for Singapore."

– Tan Tai Yong, dean, Faculty of Arts and Social Sciences, National University of Singapore

strange mix, but the two groups had similar goals. "In a way, it was the coming together of two disparate groups of people: an English-educated group of moderates and a Chinese-educated group of militants, both having the same objectives, of wanting to achieve self-government and eventual political independence for Singapore," the Southeast Asian historian said.

In the PAP, English- and Chinese-educated activists entered a marriage of convenience, with both sides aspiring to maintain the core of their own political platform.

However, cracks in the relationship started to appear as early as the 1955 election campaign.

The PAP campaign was led by Lee Kuan Yew, but on the left of the party the rising young star, Chinese-speaking Lim Chin Siong, threatened to outshine him.

According to Fong, Lim was also popular with women voters, who sought out photos of him as a keepsake.

Lee recalled later, "It was quite obvious that I was not the crowd-puller, nor were my English-educated friends. He (Lim) was."

Both Lim and Lee won their seats. However, the election victory went to the Labour Front, led by the passionate anti-colonialist David Marshall.

The PAP became the main opposition party, but this was not a state of affairs that the party's radicals liked. They found the parliamentary process slow and cumbersome, and came up with an alternative plan. In May 1955, Fong, who was leader of a bus workers' union, called for a strike that would rip apart the already delicate grouping that was the PAP.

DAVID MARSHALL

Born in Singapore on 12 March 1908, David Saul Marshal—his name was Anglicised to Marshall later—was the eldest of six children of Orthodox Jewish parents who had immigrated from Baghdad, Iraq. With a personality that was larger than life, he would eventually become Singapore's first chief minister, one of its greatest criminal lawyers and a nationalist credited with making significant contributions to the country.

Marshall studied in prestigious schools in Singapore, such as Raffles Institution, but suffered from poor health since his youth. Although he wanted to win a Queens' scholarship to study in Britain, he experienced a tubercular collapse before his examinations as a result of overwork. He was sent to recuperate in a Swiss Sanatorium, where he learned French, an attribute that he was to put to good use later in life.

At 26, Marshall made it to London to study law, in which he excelled. On his return, he started to build a legal career. When war broke out, Marshall refused to leave the country with his family, choosing instead to join the Singapore Volunteer Corps. In February 1942, he was captured by the Japanese and held at Changi Prison. Later, he was sent to work as a forced labourer in extremely harsh conditions in coal mines in Hokkaido, Japan.

Singapore Press Holdings

Chief Minister David Marshall was believed to be able to perform miracles in court, 1955.

125

After the war, Marshall returned to his legal career. Along with remarkable oratorical skills, he was a hard worker and was noted for the thoroughness of his preparation. Marshall's reputation as a criminal defence lawyer was such that he was believed to be able to perform miracles in court. The word in legal circles was that "Marshall never loses". His unparalleled success in court contributed to the government's decision to abolish the jury system, and later, in 1972, he was charged with circulating affidavits in a politically sensitive case and was suspended from the bar for six months.

Outside of work, Marshall founded and ran many societies and organisations for different causes. In 1954, he led the Labour Front, calling for immediate self-government. Charismatic and combative, his fiery speeches and sincerity in reaching out to the masses helped mobilise citizens against colonialism. He customarily appeared in public wearing a trademark white bush jacket and smoking a pipe. Marshall became the first chief minister of Singapore when the Labour Front formed a coalition government after the first Legislative Assembly election in April 1955.

After taking office, he had to address major problems such as the violent Hock Lee Bus riots, student unrest, strikes and the communist threat, and was criticised in some quarters for what was perceived as weakness. He pushed for self-government for Singapore and led a delegation to London in 1956 to hold constitutional talks. The talks failed because of disunity within the all-party delegation and because of what some regarded as Marshall's inflexible and undiplomatic approach. Angry and disappointed, Marshall resigned from the post of chief minister on June 7, 1956, and left the Labour Front the following year. In the 1959 general election he lost his seat.

Though Marshall's 14-month tenure was brief, his administration tackled tough policy issues. Marshall is credited with promoting multilingualism and emphasising the importance of learning English, which remains the basis for Singapore's education system today. He also started meet-the-people sessions, which the People's Action Party still practises; proposed a citizenship scheme for 220,000 China-born residents, which set the direction for future Singapore citizenship policies; and broached the idea of a Central Provident Fund.

A man of humane, liberal democratic instincts noted for his passion and compassion, Marshall was not a master politician, and he did not connect with citizens in an enduring way at the grassroots level. He was, more at home with the intellectual elite. After founding the Workers Party in 1957 he lost his seat in the 1959 election, but re-entered parliament after a by-election in 1961. He lost his seat in the 1963 general election.

In 1978, at the age of 70, Marshall was appointed Singapore's ambassador to Paris. For the next 15 years he performed the role of diplomat faithfully and wholeheartedly, also serving as ambassador to Portugal, Spain and Switzerland. When he returned to Singapore in 1993, Marshall was already 85, but still not prepared to retire. He joined a leading local law firm, Drew & Napier, as a consultant.

Marshall was an outspoken critic of the government, and his record of unquestionable patriotism and distinguished service to the country gave him unparalleled credibility. Yet he was also ready to give credit where it was due—even to his political adversaries.

Marshall's marriage in 1961 to an Englishwoman, Jean Gray—a social work lecturer—produced four children. On 12 December 1995, he died of lung cancer in Singapore. He was 87.

HOCK LEE BUS RIOTS

The Hock Lee Bus Riots culminated in a series of violent clashes between the police and strikers and their supporters on 12 May 1955. However, in the days leading up to what became known as "Black Thursday", trouble had already been brewing.

Workers at the Hock Lee Amalgamated Bus Company, who were members of the Singapore Bus Workers' Union (SBWU) led by Fong Swee Suan and Lim Chin Siong, were on strike in protest against new work rosters and the formation of a rival union, the Hock Lee Employees' Union (HLEU). The HLEU, which had 200 members, was formed by the bus company to respond to labour action by the SBWU.

Some workers who had been dismissed by the management after they served a strike notice, locked themselves in the company's depot on Alexandra Road and picketed the gate. Strikers also prevented buses from leaving the garages.

The striking workers were joined by busloads of students from the Chinese Middle School, who brought food and entertained the workers with songs and dances. Fong called on all bus companies to stop operating, thereby crippling Singapore's public transport system.

Other workers downed tools, in sympathy with the bus strikers or as a result of fear and confusion. The police warned the strikers that they were breaking the law, and dispersed the crowds with water hoses when their warnings were ignored.

When negotiations between the company and the SBWU broke down, the police were told to do whatever was necessary to clear the picket-lines and allow buses to pass. On 12 May, they used water cannons and tear gas to disperse a crowd that had been augmented by organised groups of students and workers arriving in buses and lorries. The crowd retaliated by throwing stones and bottles at the policemen and buses.

Fong, general secretary of the SBWU, later recalled, "That day, about 5:45 in the morning, the company sent out three or four buses. The strikers moved forward to

Singapore Press Holdings

Singapore Press Holdings

The Hock Lee Bus Riots: Police moved in on 12 May 1955, to disperse and to detain rioters. The picketers were in support of workers of Hock Lee Amalgamated Bus Company, belonging to Singapore Bus Workers' Union, who had launched a strike in late April when they were dismissed from the company.

try and stop the buses from reaching the road. The police came in with water hoses to spray the strikers. You can imagine with the riot lasting so many hours and with thousands involved, even the police lost control."

In all, four people died during the riots. One plain-clothed policeman was killed when his car was set afire by the mob, and another policeman and an American correspondent for United Press were beaten to death by the mob. A student was shot, possibly by a stray bullet, and according to local press reports at the time his wounded body was paraded around by rioters to stir emotions for hours without medical attention before he died. Thirty-one others were also injured.

"The police came in with water hoses to spray at the strikers. You can imagine, with the riot lasting so many hours, and with thousands involved, even the police lost control."

– Fong Swee Suan, secretary general,
Singapore Bus Workers' Union

Things were calmer the next day and eventually, the Hock Lee bus strike was settled through government arbitration. The settlement was favourable to the strikers, but public opinion had turned against them as a result of the violence that had accompanied the strike.

The riots demonstrated to Lee the potential for damage posed by the left-wing militants.

"They had infiltrated the trade unions, they were prepared to take direct action, mobilise the ground," said Tan Tai Yong from the National University of Singapore. "But at the same time, he (Lee) realised that he could not alienate them from the party because they had direct access to the grassroots support upon which the PAP was dependent."

Lee was quite clear as to which side he was on. His dilemma was how to stay faithful to his beliefs and yet not be perceived by grassroots supporters as betraying his fellow party workers.

The Hock Lee Bus riots played a key factor on Marshall's inability to negotiate independence from Britain. Following the riots, the chief

Lim Chin Siong (centre, garlanded) and Devan Nair (left) after being released from Changi prison on 4 June 1959.

Singapore Press Holdings

130

minister closed two schools that were closely linked to the rioters, but had to reopen them when thousands of students, backed by parents, friends and other supporters, forced their way into the buildings.

When in the spring on 1956 Marshall led an all-party delegation to London to seek independence and self-government, he was rejected, partly because of disunity among the parties and Marshall's lack of diplomacy, but also over concerns that the government couldn't keep the peace and communist influence was rising. Marshall resigned his position as chief minister soon after returning to Singapore and was replaced by his minister of labour, Lim Yew Hock.

Suspicions that communist activists were behind the riots spread through Singapore and dogged Lim Chin Siong and Fong Swee Suan for most of their lives. In a rare taped interview in 1959, Lim was asked if he were indeed a communist. "I'm sick to answer this," he replied. "This (is) not the first time I've been asked the same question. And I'm not going to spend the rest of my life to answer this question. I'm telling you categorically I'm not a communist."

In Lee's memoirs, published two years after Lim died, the former prime minister describes an encounter with Lim from 1956. "He was well-meaning and seemed deeply sincere. ... But we never developed a close friendship. Instead, we recognized each other for what we were. He knew I was not a communist, and I knew that he was one. And we accepted each other as such."

131

"I'm sick to answer this question. This (is) not the first time I've been asked the same question. And I'm not going to spend the rest of my life to answer this question. I'm telling you categorically I'm not a communist."

– Lim Chin Siong, secretary general, Barisan Sosialis

The new chief minister, Lim Yew Hock quickly gained a reputation for being tough on unionists and other activists. When renewed rioting broke out in October 1956, following a student demonstration at Chinese High School, Lim Yew Hock was quick to act. British police, tear gas and helicopters were brought to help bring the island-wide disturbance under control. Thirteen people were killed in the unrest and more than a hundred injured. The chief minister then invoked the Internal Security Act to arrest more than 1,000 people suspected to be pro-communist, anti-colonial, or unionist. Among those jailed were left-wing members of the PAP, including Lim Chin Siong and Chia Ek Tian, a member of the party's executive committee.

The British applauded Lim's heavy hand in quelling the disturbances, and after two years of negotiations approved a new constitution for Singapore, granting the island self-rule. But Lim's strong-arm tactics didn't resonate well with the majority Chinese voters in Singapore, and in the 1959 general election his party, the Singapore People's Alliance, won just four seats.

The big winner was the People's Action Party. With his main rivals in jail following the 1956 riots, Lee was the unquestioned leader of the PAP and became the country's first prime minister. Yet the victory was a mixed blessing, one that Lee called a "crown of thorns." To win popular support during the campaign, Lee had promised if elected he'd free Lim Chin Siong and other popular leftists.

"We had to release them, or otherwise we'd be seen to be unprincipled people who indulged in skulduggery."

– Lee Kuan Yew, first prime minister of Singapore

"Merger, stability, security, economic development, if we've got that, then we've got prosperity, the people's welfare."
– Lee Kuan Yew, first prime minister of Singapore

"We had to release them, or otherwise we'd be seen as unprincipled people who indulged in skulduggery, used the British to lock up our opponents," Lee said later. "So we had to release them, knowing that they're going to fight us. And that fight had to be in the open."

Within days of the PAP's election victory, crowds gathered for the eagerly anticipated release of Lim, Fong and six other political prisoners.

"When we came out we were received very warmly by the masses," said Fong. "Wherever we went, they lit firecrackers for us."

But while Lim and his colleagues were back in the PAP fold, they would not stay there long. Soon, the party would again be broken up, this time irreversibly, over the question of Singapore's future.

The British granted Malaya full independence in 1957, and the next year the British Parliament made Singapore a self-governed state, although it retained control over key areas, including foreign relations, defence and internal security.

As the country's new prime minister, Lee had promised to secure full independence from Britain, but because of the island's size and vulnerability he believed that this could only be achieved through political union with Malaya, its huge neighbour to the north.

However, there was a problem.

Malaya's leader, Tunku Abdul Rahman, did not want to upset the demographic balance that existed in his country.

133

TUNKU ABDUL RAHMAN

Born on February 8, 1903 in Alor Star, Kedah, Malaysia, Tunku Abdul Rahman Putra Alhaj was the son of the ruler of Kedah, Sultan Abdul Hamid Halim Shah. His mother was Che Manjalara, daughter of a Thai district officer.

Tunku Abdul Rahman—who later became Malaysia's first Prime Minister— is also known as *Bapa Kemerdekaan* or "Father of Independence". He led the Malayan delegation to London to negotiate the country's independence from the British. While "Tunku" is a princely title also used by other Malay aristocrats, only he is referred to as "*the* Tunku", reflecting his stature among Malaysians.

The Tunku's early education began in a Malay and English school in Alor Star, followed by a Siamese school in Bangkok and then Penang Free School.

134

Tunku Abdul Rahman (right) with Lee Kuan Yew in Singapore 1962, on his way to London for talks on Malaysia "full of hope that everything will be alright".

Singapore Press Holdings

On a Kedah government scholarship, the happy-go-lucky young man went to study at St Catharine's College, Cambridge, where he received a Bachelor of Arts degree in Law and History in 1925. While at university in Britain he had first-hand experience of racial discrimination.

According to Patrick Keith, formerly the Malaysian Government's deputy director of external information, the Tunku decided to lodge at the college and was told there was a waiting list. After a three-year wait, he asked the dean why he had still not been allocated a room. He was told that the college had been created for English gentlemen and so he could not be permitted to live there. Although the dean later capitulated and offered him a room after his father, the Sultan, intervened, the Tunku turned the offer down. He wanted all students from Malaya to be fairly treated, and not just those with the right connections. This encounter was said to have convinced him of the need to fight for equality and independence from British colonialism.

The Tunku joined the Inner Temple in London, but his studies were interrupted. At the outbreak of war he returned to Kedah, where he joined the Kedah State Civil Service. He finally went back to London to complete his law studies and was called to the bar in 1949.

When the Tunku returned to Malaya in 1949, he was appointed as a deputy public prosecutor and later as president of the Sessions Court. In August 1951, he succeeded Dato Onn bin Jaafar as president of the powerful United Malays National Organisation (UMNO).

The Tunku managed to bring Chinese and Indian political groups together with UMNO to create a coalition known as the Alliance. He led the Alliance to victory in the country's first general election, in July 1955, and became Malaya's chief minister and minister of home affairs.

135

The Tunku's successful mission to London opened the way for full independence. On 31 August 1957, at a ceremony in Kuala Lumpur he shouted "*Merdeka*!" (Independence!) seven times, and each time the crowd repeated the word, as the British flag was lowered for the last time. The Tunku became the first prime minister of Malaya and led the Alliance to landslide victories in the 1959 and 1964 general elections. One of his greatest legacies was the formation of Malaysia—a federation of Malaya, Sabah, Sarawak and Singapore—on September 16, 1963. He also became Malaysia's first prime minister.

However, two years later the Tunku decided Singapore would have to withdraw from Malaysia, which it did on 9 August 1965.

At the 1969 general election, the Alliance's majority was significantly reduced, with many seats lost to the opposition Chinese parties. This triggered demonstrations and race riots in Kuala Lumpur. Some UMNO leaders criticised Abdul Rahman's leadership at this time, and he was forced to resign as prime minister on 22 September 1970.

After acquiring a substantial stake in the Penang-based newspaper, *The Star*, the Tunku became its chairman in 1977 and wrote columns in the paper that were critical of the government.

Known for his multiracial perspective, his generosity and his amiability, the Tunku was also a keen sportsman and football fan. Keith recalled that The Tunku also enjoyed poking gentle fun at people, including his own wife, Sharifah Rodziah. Once, during a radio interview in Bangkok, he was asked if he had a message for his family. He replied that he would like his wife not to eat too much while he was away.

The Tunku died on 6 December 1990 at the age of 87 and is buried at the Royal Mausoleum, Langgar, Kedah.

U nlike Lee Kuan Yew, the Tunku was unconvinced of the benefits of Singapore's membership in Malaysia, but Lee persisted in making the case for merger.

To win support for the plan, Lee visited every part of Singapore, including rural areas, speaking directly to people, asking for their views and listening to what they had to say.

"Merger, stability, security, economic development," said Lee. "If we've got that, then we've got prosperity, the people's welfare."

Lee believed that it would be possible to deliver these things more effectively if merger with Malaya could be achieved. Singapore's left-wing opposition, however, was vehemently opposed to the plan.

In July 1961, Lim Chin Siong led a mass breakaway from the PAP and set up the left-wing Barisan Sosialis party, which was actively opposed to the merger. Lim drew widespread popular support that threatened to overwhelm the PAP and threatened to scuttle Lee's vision of independence from Britain by merging with Malaya.

137

Banners hanging at Barisan Sosialis Delta Tiong Bahru branch during prime minister Lee Kuan Yew's constituency tours of Tiong Bahru, Delta and Havelock area.

National Archives of Singapore

BARISAN SOSIALIS

Dismayed by the PAP's call for merger with Malaya and other issues, Lim Chin Siong and other left-wing party members broke away from the PAP and formed the Barisan Sosialis ("Socialist Front" in Malay) in July 1961. The new party's chairman was Lee Siew Choh, Lim its secretary general and Fong a member of the Central Executive Committee.

In the early 1960s, Barisan was the main opposition party and bitterly opposed Singapore's merger with Malaysia. The PAP accused the party of being a front for communism, a charge vehemently denied by its members.

During Operation Coldstore—a police raid to destroy the left-wing political network in the country in February 1963—Lim and Fong were among the many Barisan members arrested. The arrests had a devastating effect on the party, but it still succeeded in winning 13 out of 51 seats in the 1963 general election. Lee Siew Choh, however, failed to keep his seat. After the election, more Barisan members were arrested for alleged communist activities, including Chia Thye Poh, who became Singapore's longest serving political detainee.

After Singapore's separation from Malaysia in 1965, Lee Siew Choh claimed that Singapore's independence was "phoney" and announced that Barisan MPs would boycott parliament and "take the battle to the streets".

This strategy further fragmented the party, with several Barisan MPs resigning their parliamentary seats and leaving Barisan.

Though it organised demonstrations by Chinese-educated students and unions, Barisan was unable to regain the influence it had earlier enjoyed in the trade union movement. At the same time, the government enacted legislation which disqualified non-Singaporean citizens and people with criminal records from holding office in trade unions. All office-bearers had to be registered, and unions that took part in illegal strikes were de-registered and strikers were arrested.

A decision by Barisan to boycott the by-elections held to fill seats left open by Barisan resignations, and then to boycott the 1968 general election was a costly mistake for the party. There were no opposition MPs for the next 13 years, and the PAP enjoyed dominance in parliament for the next 30 years.

In the general elections that followed, Barisan Sosialis failed to win a seat, and in 1988 it was dissolved. Led by Lee Siew Choh, many of its members joined the Workers' Party. Lee eventually became the first non-constituency member of parliament after the 1988 general election.

139

Singapore Press Holdings

Dr Lee Siew Choh left the PAP in 1961 to form an opposition party, Barisan Sosialis and became the founding chairman.

Chapter 7

MERGER AND SEPARATION

By New Year's 1962 the pieces were in place that would lead to a final showdown between Singapore's political elites and eventually the anguished announcement that Singapore has become an independent nation.

The Barisan Sosialis began demonstrations against any merger with Malaya, calling those who favoured such a merger pro-colonialist. There were no major disturbances during this time, and by the end of the year the leftists were riding a wave of popularity. "We were very confident," Lim said. "If there's a general election, we can beat the government."

Confident, yes, but not delusional. "We had this premonition that sooner or later we would all be detained," Fong said later.

Indeed, the Tunku in Malaya was worried about the socialists and made it clear to Lee that he wanted them out of the picture.

"He wanted the burden to be carried by the British," Lee said. "And I said, 'Let's wait until after the merger.' The Tunku says, 'No. We arrest them now, or there will be no merger,' "

"He wanted the burden to be carried by the British. And I said, 'let's wait until after merger'. The Tunku says, 'No, we arrest them now, or there will be no merger'."

– Lee Kuan Yew, first prime minister of Singapore

142

Preceding page: prime minister Lee Kuan Yew in conference with labour leaders during strike threat, 1 May 1965.

"We had this premonition that sooner or later, we would all be detained.
– Fong Swee Suan, secretary general,
Singapore Bus Workers' Union

Fear of the growing influence held by the leftists and suspicions that they were a front for the communists brought together an unlikely alliance: British authorities in Singapore, Lee with his anti-colonial leanings, and the Tunku, who was reluctant to embrace Singapore because of its large Chinese population. In February 1962, the Internal Security Council, comprising members from the British, Malayan, and Singaporean government, unleashed Operation Coldstore to put the leftist radicals on ice.

All told, 113 people were arrested on suspicion of supporting communist activities and a rebellion in nearby Brunei. Among those sent to jail were Lim Chin Siong and Fong, as well as 22 other Barisan Sosialis members, 21 trade union leaders, students and journalists.

"It was after midnight," Fong said, recalling the night of his arrest. "I was in Singapore's Norfolk Road. There was an intense knocking at the door. When I opened it, standing in front of me was my neighbour. He had come to arrest me. He apologised profusely, and I said it was alright, he was just carrying out his duty."

The arrests cleared the field for the PAP to win the upcoming elections, and just as importantly removed a major barrier to Lee's plan to gain independence from the British Empire by merging with Malaya. In August, the Singapore Legislative Assembly approved the merger, and in September, the Federation of Malaysia was proclaimed.

143

But while his aim was achieved, Lee's position had moved from being number one in Singapore, to number two in Malaysia. As prime minister of the whole country, the Tunku could lay claim to ultimate authority.

According to Abdullah Ahmad, a political aide to the Tunku between 1963 and 1965, the Tunku and Lee got along very well at first, "but I think Lee Kuan Yew eventually became almost a pest to the Tunku". This, he said, was because Lee kept asking for concessions and "irritating" the Tunku.

The personality clash between the two leaders was one issue, but others would soon boil over as Singapore and Malaysia struggled to find the right balance of power. The Tunku was concerned that Singapore was demanding too much. He needed the industrial and commercial boost Singapore offered—the island accounted for about 40 percent of the federation's economy—but didn't want the political power of the Malays diluted.

"We didn't make any demands on Singapore," recalled Abdullah Ahmad, "We said, 'Look, you are part of Malaysia. You have to behave like one, like the rest of the states.' Singapore was one of the 14 component states, but Singapore was behaving like a prima donna among these, almost a nation within a nation."

One immediate problem was that the Malaysia constitution gave Malays special rights, such as job quotas, special licenses and reserved land, and it quickly became apparent that the merger agreement didn't give these privileges to Malays in Singapore.

"The Tunku had a very simple method of reminding everybody who was in charge, so the photographs, the protocol, the solid phalanx of Malays, and the few Chinese and Indians at the periphery."
– Lee Kuan Yew, first prime minister of Singapore

In mid-July, Lee met with leaders of the United Malays National Organization (UMNO) and said all Singaporeans had equal rights and the government would never allow special rights for Malays. Following the meeting, Ahmad Haji Taff, a member of UMNO's action committee, said the meeting was "an insult to Malays." Adding to the tension, earlier in the year the PAP ran unsuccessfully against the UMNO for seats in Malaysia during the general election.

With tensions growing, about 25,000 Malays gathered in Singapore's Padang on 21 July 1965, to commemorate the Prophet Muhammad's birthday. After listening to emotional speeches by the event's organisers, the crowd began parading toward Geylang.

"I was leading a PAP Muslim member's contingent, about 70 people," said Othman Wok, then-minister of social affairs. "I saw Malay youths attack onlookers on the roadside, Chinese onlookers. And I saw a Chinese old man on the bicycle who was pulled down, beaten up and his bicycle thrown into the river."

145

Along the way, some marchers became rowdy, and when a group of stragglers were told by a Chinese policeman to rejoin the procession, they turned on him. The disturbance spread rapidly to other areas, leading to a riot in which Malays attacked Chinese passerby and onlookers. A curfew was imposed to help control the volatile situation, but the violence continued for several days, with shops and cars burned. During the riots, 23 people died and 454 were injured.

A second riot took place not long afterwards, on 3 September. This time, a Malay trishaw-rider was stabbed to death at Geylang Serai, allegedly by a group of Chinese. The incident led to five days of rioting between the two ethnic groups, and a curfew was again imposed. By the time things had calmed down, 13 more people had lost their lives and 106 had been injured.

National Archives of Singapore

A race riot victim, 1964. The command riots in July and September 1965 exposed underlying tensions between Singapore's Malay and Chinese communities.

The violence between ethnic Chinese and Malays was attributed to various causes. The leaders of the UMNO blamed Lee Kuan Yew, Singapore's prime minister, and said a bottle had been thrown at the procession by an ethnic Chinese. Others pointed the finger at Indonesian and communist provocateurs who wanted Malaysia to descend into civil war.

However, Lee and several foreign observers charged that Syed Jaafar Albar, secretary general of UMNO, and other Malay extremists in the party, were responsible for a campaign of communal hatred.

The riots laid bare serious tensions between the races as well as between the leadership in Singapore and Kuala Lumpur. The fear of further violence contributed to Singapore's secession from Malaysia in 1965.

Collection of the KITLV, Leiden. The Netherlands

146

Workers pile tin from Malaya in a factory in Singapore, 1960. In the years ahead of independence, Singapore's industry was dependent on raw materials from Malaya.

"And I saw a Chinese old man on the bicycle who was pulled down, beaten up, and his bicycle thrown into the river."
— Othman Wok, eyewitness, and Singapore cabinet minister, 1963-1977

"Singapore was behaving like the prima donna among these, almost a nation within a nation."

– Abdullah Ahmad, political aide to
Tunku Abdul Rahman, 1963-65

Instead of producing unity, political union between Malaya and Singapore had produced the worst racial violence in the island's recent history.

Faced with deteriorating conditions, the Tunku concluded by August 1965 that Malay-Chinese relations had been irreparably damaged. He wanted Singapore out of the Federation and he sent a handwritten letter to the PAP leadership notifying them of his intentions.

On receipt of the letter, Othman recalled, "Everybody was rather silent, solemn."

Speaking to Discovery Channel, Lee said later, "They want us out of Malaya, out of Malaysia. So I said, 'Are they serious?' They said, 'Yes, absolutely. Otherwise there's going to be a bloodbath."

The Tunku announced the separation in a broadcast from the Malaysian capital of Kuala Lumpur.

"There have been differences between the central government and the Singapore state government, and these differences take so many forms and are of so many types that it has not been possible to resolve them," the Tunku told the television audience. "We have to break away from Singapore. ... It's the most painful piece of work that I've had to do since I've been the prime minister for the last 10 years."

Singapore's journey through the 20th century had been harrowing. But for one man in particular, the most agonising moment of all approached. Lee had been convinced that merger with Malaya was the only way for Singapore to secure viable independence; he had gambled his political credibility on this. And now, he had lost.

147

148

Prime Minister Lee Kuan Yew at a meeting with his cabinet, 1 Jan 1965.

Getty Images

"They want us out of Malaya, out of Malaysia. So I said, 'Are they serious?' They said, 'Yes, absolutely. Otherwise there's going to be a bloodbath'."

– Lee Kuan Yew, first prime minister of Singapore

"The feelings welled up. It was a difficult, emotional problem."
– Lee Kuan Yew, first prime minister of Singapore

While the Tunku's televised statement was calm and dispassionate, Lee's address on 9 August 1965 was fraught with despair. He paused often to collect himself or wipe tears from his eyes as live television cameras rolled and reporters crowding the conference room took notes.

149

"Every time we look back on the moment when we signed the agreement which severed Singapore from Malaysia, it will be a moment of anguish," the prime minister said. "You see, all my adult life I have believed in Malaysian merger and the unity of these two territories. You know these are people connected by geography, economy and ties of kinship... Would you mind if we stop for a while?"

After the conference, Lee took refuge in his seaside bungalow to chart a new course for his small and vulnerable island. Much later, reflecting on the televised announcement, Lee said, "I felt a sense of guilt for having got so many people involved in this problem, and I had to face them. ... The feelings welled up. It was a difficult, emotional problem."

Singapore was on its own.

 LION CITY-ASIAN TIGER

Chapter 8

GOING SOLO

Independence came sooner than anyone had expected. It was thrust upon Singapore when the country and its leaders were not quite ready for it. To Lee Kuan Yew, independence came as a shock.

Many Singaporeans believed their city-state was too small and vulnerable to be fully independent. There were doubts about the country's ability to transform itself into a viable nation.

The opening of the first parliament in December 1965 reinforced this notion. The head of the honour guard that was detailed to escort the prime minister from his office to parliament was a Malaysian Brigadier. Singapore did not have its own military capacity. Travelling to parliament, Lee concluded that his Malaysian military escort represented a public affirmation by the Tunku that Singapore's independence was by his "leave and license", Lee later recalled. The prime minister of Singapore did not have a single soldier under his command. "My soldiers were then under his (the Tunku's) control," said Lee.

"The prime minister of Singapore did not have a single soldier under his command. "My soldiers were then under his (the Tunku's) control."
– Lee Kuan Yew, first prime minister of Singapore

Preceding page: The Merlion, the iconic symbol of modern Singapore watches over the city skyscrapers.

SECURING SINGAPORE

After Singapore gained its independence in 1965, it was faced with several security challenges. While relations with Malaysia had been strained by the unhappy marriage and the acrimonious divorce, trouble was also brewing in Indonesia.

When Malaysia was formed, Indonesia adopted a policy of *konfrontasi,* or confrontation, aimed at disrupting the union of Malaya, Sabah, Sarawak and Singapore. *Konfrontasi* lasted from 1963 untill 1966 and involved attacks by Indonesian troops and Indonesian surrogates on Malaysian soil, mostly on the island of Borneo, but also in Singapore. Indonesian President Sukarno was opposed to the formation of Malaysia because, he argued, the new state was a British creation designed to ensure the continuation of Britain's influence in the region. The worst *konfrontasi* incident in Singapore occurred on 10 March, 1965, when a bomb exploded at MacDonald House, an office building on Orchard Road that housed the Hong Kong and Shanghai Bank. The bomb was planted by two Indonesian agents, killed three people, and wounded 33 others.

After Sukarno lost power in Indonesia, a process that began at the end of 1965, *Konfrontasi* was wound down and formally ended in August 1966. Meanwhile, further to the north, the struggle between communism and capitalism was escalating in Indo-China and anti-government insurgencies continued throughout the decade in peripheral parts of Thailand, Burma and the Philippines. The region as a whole was experiencing a period of chronic turbulence.

So it was no surprise that Singapore felt vulnerable. The police force had to be reconfigured, after being integrated with the Malaysian force during the two years of merger. The armed forces had to be built up almost from scratch.

When Singapore gained independence, its armed forces were woefully inadequate to defend the new city-state. The army was composed of two infantry battalions under British command and made up mostly of non-Singaporean troops and the Singapore Volunteer

Corps. The navy had three vessels: a captured Japanese minesweeper that served as its headquarters and two wooden patrol boats.

Secret societies, which were reinvigorated while running black markets during the Japanese Occupation, and fears of continued unrest following the 1964 race riots underscored the urgent need for a professional police force. The police force had to be authentically multi-ethnic to reflect Singapore's society and by all of the ethnic and social groups in the new country.

In addition, the development of the police force and the armed forces was viewed as a key part of creating a "Singaporean" consciousness. Citizens from Malay, Indian and Chinese backgrounds would gain a sense of solidarity and common purpose by serving in the same uniform under the same flag.

Finally, a peaceful, secure, and stable environment was needed if Singapore were to achieve rapid economic growth. Only if investors and trading partners were assured that the new country could guarantee its own peace and security could Singapore reach its objective.

156

National Archives of Singapore

Minister of the Interior and Defence Dr Goh Keng Swee arrives for opening of Signal School at Singapore Armed Forces Training Institute (Safti), 1967.

The task of building Singapore's defence and security system fell to Goh Keng Swee, who moved from the Finance Ministry and took over the new Ministry of the Interior and Defence when Singapore left Malaysia. Goh immediately set about establishing what was to be the core of the Singapore Armed Forces.

Singapore cast around for a suitable international model for its military development. Switzerland, a small republic dependent on trade and protected by a citizen army, was one possibility. However, in the end Israel was considered a better fit. Singapore reached a secret military cooperation and training agreement with Israel, and Israeli advisors trained the first batch of graduates from the Singapore Armed Forces Training Institute in June 1967. Because of sensitivities on the part of Singapore's predominantly Muslim neighbours, Singapore's military connection with Israel was never formally acknowledged and in the early years efforts were made to disguise the origin of the Israeli advisors, who were routinely described as "Mexicans" or "Indians".

Singapore's cooperation with Israel in the defence sphere reflected the similar geopolitical and military challenges facing the two countries. Both came into existence after the Second World War in unpromising circumstances and facing a significant military threat; both are small and dependent on global trade; both have strong ties in the developing world, as well as strong ties with the United States and the West. In the 1960s Israel responded positively to Singapore's request for military cooperation and in the following decades Singapore leveraged that cooperation into a defence capacity that ensured the continuing security of the city-state.

In addition to forming the nucleus of a new professional army, Goh set about establishing the volunteer People's Defence Force, and in October 1965, 3,000 volunteers signed up for the PDF.

In March 1967, mandatory national service was introduced, establishing the system which continues today, whereby 18 year olds are conscripted for a period of intensive training, after which they are placed on active reserve to support the small force of professional soldiers whenever necessary.

In addition to its military value, national service played an indispensable role in helping to forge a Singaporean identity among multiracial citizens.

"It is an equalising experience, brings all strata of people to train and live together, and that leads to mutual understanding and appreciation, which is important for a multicultural and multiracial society," said Lt. Gen. (Ret.) Winston Choo Wee Leong, Singapore's chief of defence force from 1990 to 1992. "By force of circumstance, they have to learn to live with each other, and understand that there are others in Singapore who look different, who worship differently, and who speak differently."

"Singapore is our home," Choo continued. "It is not an invention. It is a real thing. It's 660 square kilometres of land in which we live. We have nowhere else to go. This is our home."

158

National Archives of Singapore

A new recruit goes through a physical examination. Mandatory national service added to Singapore's feeling of nationhood.

"Singapore is our home. It is not an invention. It is a real thing.
– Lt. Gen. (Ret.) Winston Choo Wee Leong
Chief of Defence Force, 1990-1992

"The first thing that you do is pick up the gun, and therefore, to be a master of your own destiny. There's always a sense that unless we are strong, unless we are alert, the conditions of our existence are precarious."
– George Yeo, minister of foreign affairs, 2004

After the Singapore Armed Forces Training Institute, other facilities were established to provide technical and training support. These included the School of Basic Military Training, the School of Artillery, and the School of Signals. The armed forces also launched a scholarship programme designed to attract the best and the brightest to military careers. Those selected receive full pay while at university, and have their fees and living expenses paid. In return they are committed to serving in the armed forces for eight years after graduation.

In 1969, Singapore bought 72 French-made AMX-13 tanks, and 170 four-wheeled V200 armoured vehicles. This was the first step in a programme of continuous upgrading of equipment for the armed forces, that later included the development of a domestic weapons-manufacturing capacity.

The city-state also worked toward securing regional alliances.

In October 1971, the Anglo-Malayan Defence Agreement was replaced by the Five Power Defence Arrangement between Singapore, the United Kingdom, Australia, New Zealand and Malaysia. All members would consult each other in the event of any threat of attack against Singapore or Malaysia. Also under this agreement, member countries could conduct a wide variety of shared military activities, including annual joint military exercises and the maintenance of an Integrated Air Defence System.

159

I-Hawks Sam System Fire Units on display at Singapore Armed Forces (SAF) Historical Exhibition, Paya Lebar Airport.

NATIONAL SERVICE

A National Service Bill was passed in 1953 by the colonial Legislative Assembly as part of the process leading towards Singapore's self-government. In May 1954, some 25,000 men registered for national service. These men were deployed on guard duties and security patrols. This marked the beginning of national service in Singapore, today still an important part of nation-building.

When Singapore gained independence in August 1965, its military force was far from an effective deterrent, particularly at a time when neighbouring Indonesia was actively engaged in hostilities that included a bombing campaign in Singapore. It was always clear that, not least because of its small population and land area, Singapore's military posture must be defensive. The military doctrine in the early years was analogous to that of the "poison shrimp" which can be eaten, but which then wreaks havoc. The object was to make any attempted assault on Singapore so costly to the aggressor that such a course of action would be rejected out of hand.

National service was seen as one of the pillars of nation-building. It would help instil a sense of belonging and citizenship in Singapore and foster social cohesion. This was particularly needed at a time when national identity had not yet evolved and when Singapore citizens often looked to their own cultural and ethnic roots for their sense of identity.

In March 1967, the national service (Amendment) Bill was passed requiring all male citizens to report for national service when they reached the age of 18. Registration reminders were sent to more than 9,000 men born between 1 January and 30 June 1949. Because of limited facilities and trainers, only 10 per cent were initially selected to do

161

full-time national service. The first batch of full-time servicemen served between two to three years, followed by 10 years of reserve service while undergoing periodic training until the age of 40. The remaining 90 per cent would be in part-time service in the People's Defence Force, the Special Constabulary or the Vigilante Corps for 12 years. Today, unless exempted for medical reasons, all Singaporean males are conscripted to join the armed forces at age 18 for two years; some early school-leavers are enlisted at age 16 or 17.

National service enlistees who are operationally fit go through basic military training for a period of 9 to 26 weeks depending on their physical condition. Those who are not operationally fit undergo modified training programmes.

After basic training, enlistees are posted to combat, service or technical vocations or selected for officer or specialist training, depending on their performance and aptitude. Others are posted to the Air Force, Navy, Police or Civil Defence Force.

On completion of two years as full-time national service-men, they serve in the reserve for a maximum of 40 days every year until the age of 40, or the age of 50 for officers. In January 1994, the term "reservists" was changed to "operationally ready NSmen", to reflect the key role they play as frontline and opera-tionally-ready troops.

During the training cycle of 13 years, NSmen return for in-camp training, including a minimum of nine stints under "high key training", sessions lasts of at least seven days of strenuous activities. During this time, NSmen are taught new skills and kept updated on the latest operational doctrines and equipment.

NSmen account for the bulk of Singapore Armed Forces manpower. While the strength of the full-time army is 50,000, the army's total strength is boosted to 350,000 with the mobilisation of all NSmen.

National Archives of Singapore

First recruits of National Services taking the oath
of allegiance in July 1954.

163

"Today, every young Singaporean man, his family, his friends, consider it very natural that the young man should perform that most demanding and noble duty of a citizen—bearing arms in the defence of the country," former Prime Minister Goh Chok Tong noted at an event to mark the 35th anniversary of the introduction of national service. "National service is a rite of passage for every able-bodied Singaporean male. The sons of our early national servicemen are now doing national service. Unlike the early days, parents understand the rationale for national service. They accept without hesitation the need for their sons to take up arms for Singapore."

PEACETIME ACTIVITIES

The Singapore Armed Forces (SAF) has played an effective peacetime role. In 2003, when an epidemic of Severe Acute Respiratory Syndrome (SARS) broke out in Singapore, the military was enlisted in the fight against the highly contagious disease, identifying and tracing all who might have been exposed to the virus in order to quarantine them. In total, some 1,500 people were quarantined in alternative housing. The SAF helped set up the Ministry of Health Operations Centre and Contact Tracing Centre within 48 hours and assembled a case-management system and link-analysis system for contact-tracing in less than 10 days. SAF medics also helped screen air travellers,

In December 2005, Singapore's military was again deployed quickly and effectively, mounting its largest humanitarian effort to date after a massive earthquake off the western coast of Sumatra on 26 December triggered a devastating tsunami that wrought death and destruction along the coasts of Indonesia, Thailand and Sri Lanka. Singapore sent Humanitarian Assistance Support Group personnel, comprising soldiers, SAF medical corps, combat engineers, drivers, commandos, naval divers, signallers and SAF logisticians, and relief supplies to Meulaboh in Indonesia.

164

DISPLAYING POWER

A year after Singapore was thrust into independence, the government organised an anniversary celebration at the Padang.

Intended as a popular morale booster, the National Day Parade on 9 August 1966 began in the morning hours with President Yusof Ishak and cabinet ministers seated on the steps of City Hall to witness a march-past by several platoons of the volunteer People's Defence Force. The PDF contingent was made up of civilian soldiers, civil servants, members of parliament and ministers who had been put through a crash officer-training course, community leaders representing all races bearing banners and slogans, units from trade unions, the PAP, statutory boards, and the police and fire brigade. The parade continued from the Padang through Chinatown to Tanjong Pagar and was televised live. It proved to be an effective exercise in fostering a sense of national pride among Singaporeans.

"The Malaysians might not have been in awe of our military capability, but they could not but be impressed by the determination and the spirit with which we were building up our defence forces to protect our fledgling state," Lee Kuan Yew remarked in his memoirs.

At the fourth National Day Parade, in 1969, Singapore showed off the AMX-13 tanks and V200 armoured vehicles it had recently acquired. Among the guests were the defence ministers from Malaysia, Britain, Australia and New Zealand, countries that would soon join Singapore in the Five Power Defence Arrangement.

165

Army contingent marching in the National Day parade during week-long celebrations to mark the first anniversary of Singapore's independence in 1966.

"It had a dramatic effect on the people in Johore when they saw it on television that night, and elsewhere in Malaysia the following day in their newspapers, which carried photos of the tanks," Lee Kuan Yew recalled. "The Malaysians had no tanks then. At my dinner that night, [Tun Abdul] Razak told [Goh] Keng Swee that many people in Malaysia were concerned over our armour, but he himself was not. He said there was anxiety in Johore whether Singapore intended to invade the state and suggested that [Lim] Kim San as defence minister should go to Kuala Lumpur to convince people that Singapore's intentions towards Malaysia were not hostile."

Over the years, the National Day Parade has evolved into an elaborate and entertaining visual display, often making use of the latest high-tech multimedia technology. Tickets to the parade are free, but because of high demand (people have been known to queue for tickets for as long as 36 hours before they become available), the government set up an electronic balloting system in 2003. Citizens and foreigners who are permanent residents can enter a lottery for tickets using their email address or mobile phone number.

Establishing a fledgling army was the start of a long road, and it was just one element in a complex evolution that transformed Singapore from a Lion City into Asian tiger.

Tanks roll down Singapore streets during a rehearsal for the country's National Day Parade, 2005. The annual parade, marking Singapore's independence, quickly became a showcase for the country's modern military.

166

Associated Press

"The Malaysians might not have been in awe of our military capability, but they could not but be impressed by the determination and the spirit with which we were building up our defence forces to protect our fledgling state."

– Lee Kuan Yew, first prime minister of Singapore

CREATING A NEW ECONOMY

Singapore's untimely independence in 1965 meant not only that it had to scramble to defend itself; but also that the country had to reconfigure its economy. In the years before the merger, rapid economic growth had been achieved through strategic government investment in housing and industrial development. However, Singapore's economy had always been viewed—and organised— on the basis of the island's industrial and commercial relationship with Malaya. Rubber and tin, for example, were produced in Malaya and then transported to Singapore to be processed and exported. Singapore had industrial capacity, but no natural resources. This symbiotic economic relationship intensified during the two years in which Singapore was part of Malaysia, and was then suddenly stopped in its tracks.

Britain announced plans to withdraw all its military forces from Asia by 1971, dealing the country's econo-my yet another blow. At the time the British forces in Singapore accounted for around 40,000 civilian jobs and military spending in the country accounted for about 15 per cent of Singapore's GNP. Britain's withdrawal threatened to be an economic catastrophe.

167

"British forces here buy goods from the provision shops, the dry cleaners, bars, hire maids, et cetera. We were in a pickle," Lee said later.

However, the island's fortunes were again lifted as a consequence of events in China. The outbreak of the Cultural Revolution in China created a climate of uncertainty that scared many international investors away from Hong Kong and Taiwan. Looking for alternative manufacturing and trading centres in Asia, they found Singapore.

In the late 1960s the first international electronic companies set up basic assembly lines in Singapore producing circuit boards and silicon chips. By the 1980s, Singapore was one of the leading centres in Asia for the production of consumer electronics.

While many Asian countries looked at multinationals as "evil companies", Singapore welcomed them with open arms, said Philip Yeo, chairman of the Economic

Development Board from 1986 to 2001. "I used to tell my colleagues that we are in the hospitality business," he said. Singapore gave investors complete freedom to run their operations, and allowed 100 per cent foreign ownership, while other countries restricted foreigners to minority shares of domestic assets. In addition, government policy towards domestic as well as foreign companies, was characterised by a *laissez faire* approach that provided companies with maximum freedom within an efficiently regulated marketplace.

Just as Raffles had attracted merchants to 19th century Singapore by offering a tax-free haven, the government now set about making Singapore the most business-friendly country in the world.

The country's economy and attractiveness to foreign investors was also helped by harmonious labour relations. A 2003 report by the US Department of Labor notes, "Much of Singapore's economic success can be tied to its human resources policies." Since the 1960s, the Singapore government worked to create flexible labour conditions, for example by easing regulations on working hours and dismissals. Workers, in exchange, received additional protection, such as unemployment benefits and paid sick leave.

Smooth relations were also helped by the National Trade Union Congress' (NTUC) close ties to the PAP and the government. The NTUC has consistently supported government recommendations on wages, even when the recommendations called for wage cuts in tough economic times, which the trade association sees as necessary to preserve jobs during downturns. The vast majority of Singapore trade unions are affiliated with the NTUC.

In 1968, the government enforced new labour laws that greatly restricted the right to strike. When companies did encounter strikes, the new legislation made it possible to threaten strikers with dismissal. "We restart with a new workforce, carefully screened, so no troublemaker is re-employed," Lee Kuan Yew remarked.

With the promise of low taxes, competitive labour rates and a well-trained workforce, Singapore became a magnet for multinational investors.

BIRTH OF THE ECONOMIC DEVELOPMENT BOARD

Singapore's economic and industrial strategy was the brainchild of prime minister Lee Kuan Yew, finance minister Goh Keng Swee and Albert Winsemius, a Dutch United Nations development economist who served as chief economic advisor to the Singapore government from 1961 to 1984. Winsemius recommended the expansion of labour-intensive manufacturing industries and thereafter their upgrade to capital-intensive, high-value-add production.

He also recommended Singapore's development as a financial centre and transport hub and, among other things, encouraged government expenditure on public housing, arguing that effective social welfare policies would make Singapore a more attractive investment destination for international capital. Winsemius recommended the establishment of an Economic Development Board to spearhead Singapore's industrialisation.

Philips launched its first Asia-Pacific DVD manufacturing facility in Singapore to serve the worldwide market and the only one outside Europe, 1999.

169

Associated Press

In 1961, with a budget of S$100 million, the Economic Development Board (EDB) was set up. It had four divisions: investment promotion, finance, a projects and technical consulting service, and industrial facilities. It had the status of an autonomous government agency, with a board comprising members from business and other agencies. It also had an international advisory board that included executives of major foreign companies located in Singapore.

The EDB was tasked with persuading international investors to do business in Singapore and with developing a global network through which to market and sell Singapore products. The EDB opened offices in Hong Kong and New York in the 1960s, expanding its network to other parts of the United States and Asia, as well as Europe in the following decade.

The EDB's signature development project during the 1960s was the Jurong Industrial Estate, a massive area of swampland on the southwestern corner of the island, which was cleared for factory use starting from 1961. By 1968, more than 150 factories were operating in Jurong and almost 50 more were under construction. The project, which some critics viewed as an expensive white elephant, got off to a slow start. However, the various infrastructure components—land clearance, utilities installation, port and road connections—were all completed on schedule and when the American giant, Texas Instruments (TI) established a plant in Jurong in 1968 to assemble semiconductors it opened the floodgates to more investors.

The EDB spent four months in talks with TI, during which it sought to persuade the American company that Singapore was by far the most-competitive location for its proposed semiconductor and integrated circuit

170

The paquebot "France" in the port of Singapore, 1972.

Roger-Viollet/AFP

manufacturing plant. The agency made sure that the commitments it had made to TI were honoured, and within just 50 days of TI's decision to make a S$6 million investment, the plant went into operation, marking the beginning of the electronics industry in Singapore.

By the 1970s, Singapore had managed to eradicate unemployment. The EDB continued to woo investors, emphasising the country's attractions as a rapid start-up location—where factories could be built to order and where a highly skilled workforce was available.

Meanwhile, an ambitious programme of vocational training was introduced, designed to turn out workers and managers imbued with a commitment to hard work and the pursuit of excellence.

"These are value systems that we have got to inculcate into the young people. We don't train people to be Greek mythologists or in English or ancient literature. Everything is about engineering, science and technical skills—skills by which they can earn a living," said Yeo.

The emphasis on training was a direct and pragmatic response to Singapore's lack of natural resources. Its single greatest natural asset has always been its population, and the economic development strategy was based on enhancing labour and management skills. Among other initiatives, the Overseas Training Programme was launched in 1971 to place Singaporean apprentices in premium workplaces worldwide. Under the programme, Joint Government Training Centres were set up with Tata in India, Philips in the Netherlands and Rollei in Germany.

171

"We don't train people to be Greek mythologists or in English or ancient literature. Everything is about engineering, science and technical skills-skills by which they can earn a living."
– Philip Yeo, chairman, Economic Development Board 1986-2001

THE WESTERN PIONEERS

Many companies that are household names around the world pioneered their East Asian operations in Singapore and were instrumental in kick-starting the country's rapid economic growth, and its development as an Asian Tiger.

To help spur foreign investment, the Economic Development Board (EDB) offered companies pioneer certificates if they opened factories on the island that made products that hadn't been manufactured there before or had been manufactured only in small quantities. Textiles, electronics, metals and plastics were among the industries being sought, and those companies awarded a pioneer certificate were given tax breaks, training subsidies and could import capital goods and raw materials duty free. There was also the expectation that the rules of the game would not change frequently, giving foreign multinationals a stable environment. In 1961, 12 pioneer certificates were awarded, but within a decade that number had risen to almost 400.

Singapore's breakthrough came with Texas Instruments' S$6 million investment in 1968. The plant was officially opened on 4 July 1969, producing semiconductors and integrated circuits for global export. Soon afterwards, Texas Instruments' rival, Hewlett-Packard (HP) began operations in Singapore. The HP venture began in a small rented factory with just 62 employees. By 1977, HP had acquired its own factory and employed a staff of 1,500. In 1984 a Singaporean—Koh Boon Hwee—was appointed to head HP Singapore. In 1970, General Electric (GE) set up six different facilities in Singapore to develop electrical and electronic products, circuit breakers and electric motors. Within 10 years, GE had become the country's single largest private employer.

The first European multinational to establish manufacturing operations in Singapore was SGS-Thomson, which launched an assembly plant in 1969 to assemble transistors. NEC was among the first in a wave of major Japanese companies to set up manufacturing operations in Singapore from the late 1960s onwards.

THIS GIRL'S
IN LOVE
WITH YOU

This girl's in love
with you
Or so it seems
the way she smiles
and cares

Gentle hostess
serene
in her sarong kebaya
serving a banquet
in the sky

This girl
this girl of SIA

Chapter 9

MADE IN
SINGAPORE

SINGAPORE
AIRLINES
The Singapore successor to MSA

...es (SIA) serves half the world and more, backed by 25 years' experience and an all-Boeing fleet.

TOKYO OSAKA
TAIPEI
HONG KONG
LONDON FRANKFURT
ZURICH
ROME ATHENS
BANGKOK MANILA
PENANG SAIGON
BOMBAY KUALA LUMPUR KOTA KINABALU
BRUNEI

As Singapore moved successfully along the economic development path with the help of massive investment from incoming multinationals, Lee Kuan Yew was determined that the country would not develop into a branch economy, where, at the first sign of an economic slowdown, companies would close their operations and relocate elsewhere. It was therefore imperative that Singaporean workers and managers learn from the multinationals they were working for. If enough expertise and capital could be accumulated, indigenous Singaporean companies could begin to compete in the international marketplace.

As part of this process, the government moved aggressively into the commercial sector on its own account. Civil servants were given intensive management training and then placed in charge of new companies set up by the government.

One of the first such companies was Singapore Airlines (SIA), which emerged in 1972 from the breakup of Malaysia-Singapore Airlines. The new airline was conceived and operated as a money-making venture that would develop a market niche on purely commercial criteria. It wasn't limited to servicing Singapore's small domestic aviation market, and it wasn't viewed as a "prestige" project, though it was understood that as the national flag carrier its success would reflect positively on the country as a whole.

"This is not a government that is willing or able to support a flag carrier for the sake of a flag carrier," Lee explained later.

Preceding page: The Singapore Girl dominates in a typical 1970s advertisement for Singapore Airlines.

Lim Chin Beng, the airline's managing director in its first decade, recalled Lee Kuan Yew's pointed remark at a dinner to mark Singapore Airlines' inauguration. "He said, we are not running Singapore Airlines as a prestige organisation for the government. So, if you don't make money, I will close you down without hesitation."

Everyone at the dinner knew Lee meant what he said. "So that was really a great incentive for us to make Singapore Airlines profitable from the very beginning," Lim said.

While the aviation industry at that time was still highly regulated, Singapore Airlines did not want to be governed by the rules set down by the International Air Transport Association, (IATA), rules that micromanaged such minutia as how much to charge for earphones and how thick sandwiches should be. Singapore Airlines resigned from IATA and set its own standards, giving for instance free drinks and earphones. "That went down very well with the passengers," Lim said.

The airline's in-flight service quickly gave it a competitive edge and even began to establish benchmarks for the rest of the industry.

177

Jonathan Drake/Bloomberg Getty Images

*Singapore - May 05: Valuair Ltd. chairman and chief executive Lim Chin Beng poses
in front of one of his company's planes at Singapore's Changi Airport before the
budget carrier's inaugural flight on Wednesday, May 5, 2004.*

The airline's icon, the Singapore Girl, builds on a corporate emphasis on training that rivals that of any of its competitors. "When our girls provide good service, they look as if they are doing this naturally," said Lim. "Actually, they are doing this according to very strict procedures."

Lim ascribed the success of the company's in-flight service to a legacy of Asian hospitality and English-language education: "It is this combination of the Asian and Western culture in the Singapore population that is so important."

The Singapore Girl has become for many a symbol of Singapore itself—a mix of Western efficiency and Eastern promise.

Lee Kuan Yew recalled congratulating the airline's management on the success of the Singapore Girl campaign, "but at the same time, that was quite a problem because for the Singapore girl to remain attractive, she's got to stay on the right side of the 30s, and if you allow the kind of trade union rules to keep a matron on till she's 40, then you haven't quite caught that bloom of youth, freshness, eagerness.

So very early on we made quite sure that everybody understood that we play by a different set of rules."

"He said, we are not running Singapore Airlines as a prestige organisation for the government. So, if you don't make money, I will close you down without hesitation."

– Lim Chin Beng, managing director,
Singapore Airlines 1972–1982

THE SINGAPORE GIRL

In 1972, Ian Batey, a young British-born advertising executive, was working on the Malaysia-Singapore Airlines account. When the company broke up and Singapore Airlines was formed, Batey approached the new airline's management and explained that he intended to start his own advertising agency and wanted Singapore Airlines to be his first client. With the birth of Batey Ads came the Singapore Girl. Batey Ads would go on to build an international reputation on the back of its successful creation of the Singapore Airlines icon.

With her immaculate makeup, neatly coiffed hair and figure-hugging *kebaya* (a traditional outfit worn by women in some parts of Southeast Asia), the Singapore Girl fronted most of the advertisements for Singapore's national carrier. She was often seen in exotic locations greeting local people with a warm smile or playing with children. The conventional focus of airline advertising in the 1970s was on flight-safety. However, Batey established a new trend of "mood" advertising in the industry, showing how flying with Singapore Airlines was a positive overall experience.

"We wanted to convey what you really get when you go on board the plane, and the Singapore Girl is a true reflection of the heart of the SIA in-flight service," Batey told the *Straits Times*.

In 1993, the Singapore Girl joined 400 famous figures from history at Madam Tussaud's waxworks in London. This was the first time that a character created for an advertising campaign had been put on display at Tussaud's.

The selection process for Singapore Airlines flight stewardesses was exacting—applicants had to be younger than 26, speak fluent English, and, according to the airline's own recruitment ads, be "slim and attractive with a good complexion and a warm personality".

179

About 20 per cent of those who apply are hired and once selected, the rigourous training begins. Learning to smile, to say "hello" to everyone, to deal with difficult customers with grace and calm, was all part of the training, as were courses in makeup and personal grooming. Rules about hairdos—no root perms, afros or boyish crops, no fringes touching eyebrows, or sides touching the face—had to be strictly followed. Stewardesses could be repri-manded for having chipped nails or failing to wear lipstick.

Etiquette classes imparted lessons in deportment and alerted in-flight trainees to social gaffes such as asking passengers how much they had paid for clothes or accessories. The girls also had to complete a British Council English course designed to instil clear diction and proper intonation.

As a marketing icon, few can doubt the success of the Singapore Girl, but she has had her detractors. Critics complain the image is sexist and perpetuates the stereotype of Asian women as meek and obedient.

In early 2007, Singapore Airlines reviewed its overall advertising strategy and, following a protracted evaluation process, decided to drop Batey Ads in favour of the international advertising giant, TBWA. The decision caused a furore in Singapore, with popular concern expressed over the future of the Singapore Girl. The reaction highlighted the fact that the Singapore Girl had evolved from an airline marketing tool to a national icon.

After a heated media debate about whether the Singa-pore Girl should be retired, the airline issued a statement say-ing, "The strong support from our customers globally for the iconic Singapore Girl, as a representation of the high service standards we aim to deliver, is very much appreciated. Singapore Airlines takes this opportunity to reassure our customers and supporters the world over that the Singapore Girl icon will remain, and there will be no change to the hallmark sarong *kebaya* uniform."

Singapore Airlines cabin crew in Changi Airport's Terminal Three.

The airline's renowned in-flight service was also matched by a reputation for having young aircraft and for renewing its fleet more regularly than any other major airline. Recalling the company's early practice of buying as many as 10 747s at a time, Lim Chin Beng said "that was unheard of. People thought we were crazy."

Singapore Airline remains one of the most successful carriers in the world, and has bucked the international trend whereby state-owned carriers have generally failed to keep up with private competitors. This has been a characteristic of the Singaporean economy as a whole, with state-owned companies—adhering ruthlessly to commercial performance targets and management practices—dominant in all the major sectors, including telecommunications, manufacturing, aviation and heavy industry.

Singapore Airlines became the first commercial airline to fly the double-decker A380, the world's biggest passenger plane, when it began service to Sydney on 25 October 2007.

SINGAPORE CHANGI AIRPORT

Central to the growth of Singapore Airlines was the country's airport. By the 1970s, the airport at Paya Lebar just east of the central business district was facing congestion problems, forcing the government to consider immediate options for expansion.

Two options were on the table: expand the existing airport at Paya Lebar, or build a new airport somewhere else. A team of British consultants recommended in 1972 that a second runway be built at Paya Lebar. This was reviewed in the light of the 1973 oil crisis by a team of American consultants. The Americans, however, reached the same conclusion—that expansion at Paya Lebar would be the most time and cost efficient way to deal with the congestion problems.

However, Lee Kuan Yew was not convinced. He had concerns that noise pollution from a larger airport at Paya Lebar would impact residents in the city and surrounding areas. Consequently, he appointed Howe Yoon Chong, then chairman of the Port of Singapore Authority, to head a top-level committee to undertake a thorough reappraisal of the project.

183

Howe's committee reported that the first runway at the new location, Changi at the eastern end of the island, could be completed by 1980 and a second by 1982, whereas a second runway at Paya Lebar, contrary to earlier reports, could only be completed by 1984 because of the need to divert Serangoon River and to compact the soil on the riverbed.

But the odds were still stacked against building a new airport at Changi, as it would cost S$1 billion, and it would be necessary to spend $400 million to expand Paya Lebar in the interim. In gloomy global economic conditions, this was a huge bill.

The government decided to proceed with a new airport at Changi.

"The airport and the pleasant 20-minute drive into the city made an excellent introduction to Singapore, the best S$1.5 billion investment we ever made."

– Lee Kuan Yew, first prime minister of Singapore

Construction at Changi International Airport, showing the field's iconic control tower.

184

"Changi is a beautiful site on the eastern most corner of the island," Lee recalled. "The approach to the city from the east coast runs along a new 20-kilometre expressway built on land reclaimed from the sea, with no problems of congestion, beautiful glimpses of the sea on one side and vistas of HDB (Housing and Development Board) estates and private condominiums on the other. The airport and the pleasant 20-minute drive into the city made an excellent introduction to Singapore, the best S$1.5 billion investment we ever made. It helped Singapore become the hub airport of the region."

Construction began immediately after the government decided to build the new airport on the site of an old air base. Workers faced special challenges, however. Hundreds of buildings were demolished to make way for Changi Airport. Thousands of graves were exhumed and relocated, and a massive tract of swampland was drained and the land reclaimed.

Changi Airport opened 1 July 1975, and in its first year it handled 8.1 million passengers, compared to an annual capacity of 4 million passengers at the old Paya Lebar Airport. During that first year, Changi also moved 193,000 tons of air freight, and altogether 65,054 flights arrived or departed from the facility.

By 2008, 33 years later, the airport had undergone several facelifts and expansions. Four terminals were in operation, including a budget terminal, and another was planned to be opened before 2023. The airport covered 13 square kilometres, about two thirds of which had been reclaimed from the sea, and it had two parallel runways, each four kilometres long, and a total of 25.3 kilometres of taxiway. Also in 2008, the airport handled almost 38 million passengers, saw almost 232,000 aircraft come and go, and moved 1.85 million tons of airfreight.

Beyond these statistics, however, the airport has also gained a global reputation as one of the world's best for passengers, winning many awards for customer service. In 2009, *USA Today* published an article asking the question: What makes Singapore's Changi Airport so charming? Its answer was good ambience, creative amenities, and staff that gives as much attention to passengers on the ground as Singapore Girls give to those in the air.

This Singapore model has been seen by many as a form of successful socialism, but one tempered by hard-nosed and astute economics. A notable example of this style of socialism is Singapore's approach to housing and other industries.

SINGAPORE CHANGI AIRPORT

By 2008, Changi Airport was handling almost 38 million passengers a year and encompassed 13 square kilometres of land.

From its early years, the Singapore government was been involved in many sectors of the economy. In some places, it worked with private investors on areas critical to the island's economic development, and in others it jumped in as sole investor in fields in which private investors didn't have the necessary capital or expertise. Many of these early enterprises have become household words in the city-state

One example is the Development Bank of Singapore, known as DBS Bank, Southeast Asia's largest by assets. The bank was founded in 1968 as a vehicle for long-term credit for industrial development projects. The government owned 49 per cent of the bank, with the remainder in private hands. Over the next four decades, the bank evolved into a multipurpose consumer bank and the government had divested to less than 30 per cent interest. In 2008, about two thirds of the bank's profits came from Singapore, and most the rest from Hong Kong. It had operations in more than a dozen other markets.

Another early investment by the Singapore government was Neptune Orient Lines (NOL), which was founded by the government in 1968 as the country's national shipping line. In the beginning, the shipping company had just five ships and faced stiff competition from European players that had dominated the seas for more than a century. By the mid-1970s, the company had a fleet of 20 ships and, with Goh Chok Tong, the future prime minister, as managing director, turned in its first profitable year.

Also in the 1970s, Neptune Orient Lines began making investments in a new technology, container shipping, in which goods are pre-loaded into uniform-sized containers. The moved had helped the company expand its regional business, as well as Asia-Europe routes. In the 1980s, it offered shares to the public and in 1997 it took over the US company APL, formerly American President Lines. By 2008, with the government still owning about two thirds of the company, Neptune Orient Lines was operating about 130 ships and sat among the global leaders in container shipping and logistics.

Much as Changi Airport is a part of Singapore Airlines' history, the Singapore Port has a symbiotic relationship with the Port of Singapore Authority. The authority was established in 1964 to replace the Singapore Harbour Board in operating Singapore's ports. It was also among the world's first port authorities to invest heavily in container technology, opening the first of a new generation of container berths in Tanjong Pagar in 1972. The authority became a government-owned entity, PSA Corporation Ltd, in 1997. Today, PSA runs facilities around the globe and its container terminals in Singapore are the world's busiest.

While the stereotype for state companies world-wide suggests businesses that are slow, inefficient, and surviving through government largess, many of Singapore's state companies defy this image. Observers credit the success of Singapore state-controlled enterprises to officials who understood that successful businesses are run by professional managers and not by people cashing in political favours and to an unflinching focus on profitability. And while it's hard to argue with success, critics of the system suggest that by being so entangled in the market, the government squeezes out private entrepreneurs.

187

By Courtesy of PSA Corporation Limited

PSA's Keppel Terminal in southern Singapore. By 2005, the Port of Singapore was the busiest container port in the world.

HOUSING THE PUBLIC

Along with coaxing economic growth from the small island, Singapore's leaders also had to worry about how to house its expanding population. Indeed, this was a problem that pre-dated the country's own independence. Already in 1959, during his term as prime minister of the Crown Colony, Lee Kuan Yew was faced with a severe housing shortage.

The majority of Singaporeans were living amid squalid conditions in crowded squatter areas concentrated in the city centre. And the population was growing rapidly, with immigration making further demands on scarce housing stock. Singapore's housing shortage had reached crisis proportions with an estimated 16,000 new homes needed annually. The government was well aware that it had to build as many flats as possible as quickly as possible and in 1960 it created the Housing and Development Board (HDB). The board's remit was to accelerate and expand the modest housing programmes that had been implemented during the previous decade. The HDB was chaired by Lim Kim San, with Howe Yoon Chong as chief executive officer, Teh Cheang Wan as chief architect, J R Stevens as structural engineer and Alan Choe as town planner. Between 1960 and 1963, the board had built 30,906 flats, almost 8,000 more than the 22,115 flats the HDB's British predecessor had built in 32 years. By 1965, it had built 54,000 flats, exceeding the 50,000-flat target of its First Five-Year Building Programme.

Moving people into high-rise buildings was not easy. New HDB residents, particularly those who had relocated from rural areas, had to adjust to their new surroundings. Some continued to use

188

National Archives of Singapore

Kampong residents, 1963

kerosene lamps even though there was electricity in the new HDB flats. Others climbed the stairs because they were afraid to take the lifts. In his memoirs, Lee Kuan Yew recalled instances of residents rearing pigs in their apartments, coaxing the animals up and down the stairs. One family, a couple with 12 children, who moved into a new HDB flat at Old Airport Road, brought a dozen chickens and ducks to rear in the kitchen. The mother built a wooden gate at the kitchen entrance to stop the creatures from entering the living room. In the evenings, the children would look for earthworms and insects in the grass patches outdoors to feed their livestock. They did this for 10 years until they moved to another flat.

Instead of renting public housing, as had been the norm in some parts of Britain, Singaporeans were encouraged to become home-owners. In this way, Lee sought to avoid what he regarded as a culture of dependency. In due course, the Singapore model of social housing, adapted from the British system, found its way back to Britain. The former British Prime Minister Margaret Thatcher, a long-time admirer of Lee Kuan Yew, was inspired by the Singaporean model, and launched a programme to encourage tenants in the UK to buy their own homes.

In 1964, Lee Kuan Yew launched a Home Owner-ship for the People scheme. He explained the scheme's rationale, "So we decided that we would give everybody a chance to own their home."

Under the Scheme, the HDB provided low interest loans. However, few Singaporeans could afford the down-payment of 20 per cent of the flat's price. So in 1968, the Central Provident Fund (CPF) Act was amended to allow people to use CPF, the governments mandatory savings plan, for the down-payment as well as housing loan repayments. The Home Ownership Scheme also had a larger purpose. Lee believed the flats provided an incentive for Singaporeans to work hard; they would become property owners and they would have a stake in the overall security and stability of the country that would protect that property. He believed that national service, might not be viable if Singaporeans did not feel they had a tangible stake to defend.

"After independence in 1965, I was troubled by Singapore's completely urban electorate. I had seen how voters in capital cities always tended to vote against the government of the day and was determined that our householders should become home owners, otherwise we would not have political stability," Lee wrote in his memoirs. "My other important motive was to give all parents whose sons would have to do national service a stake in the Singapore their sons had to defend. If the soldier's family did not own their home, he would soon conclude he would be fighting to protect the properties of the wealthy".

Queen Elizabeth II serves a sepak takraw player with a rattan ball during her tour around a housing estate in Singapore, March 2006.

After the initial housing crisis had been dealt with, the HDB embarked on ambitious programmes to provide more variety and choice. By the early 1970s, larger four-room and five-room flats were being built. Over the years, flats in different shapes and sizes were built to suit the different income and lifestyle requirements of Singaporeans.

These included one- and two-room flats for lower-income families, studio apartments for the elderly, three- and four-room flats for middle-income earners, and larger five-room and executive flats for higher-income households and extended families. In 1995, the HDB launched flats with condominium facilities.

Over time, HDB estates became more sophisticated. Landscaped greenery, multi-storey car parks, playgrounds and fitness corners, easy access to train stations, neighbourhood shopping centres, hawker centres, wet markets, schools, libraries, cinemas and recreational and entertainment facilities became characteristic elements of an HDB neighbourhood, managed by the residents themselves.

The government was also very aware of the need to integrate the different ethnic groups in these estates. In 1989, an ethnic integration policy was introduced to promote racial harmony in HDB estates. Ethnic proportions in each block and neighbourhood were subject to quotas to ensure a balanced mix of racial groups. This would prevent racial enclaves from forming, thus maintaining racial harmony and social cohesion.

As new estates came on stream, older estates were upgraded to provide new facilities, such as lifts on every floor, playgrounds, parks and fitness corners. The Main Upgrading Program was introduced in 1990 for major upgrading work on estates more than 18 years old. To cater for new estates that nonetheless required some upgrading, the Interim Upgrading Programme was launched in 1993.

Today, more than 80 per cent of Singaporeans live in some 900,000 HDB flats. Of these, 90 per cent are home owners, compared to a home-ownership rate of less than 10 per cent in the early 1960s. Singapore now has one of the highest rates of home ownership in the world.

191

Singapore Tourism Board

More than 80 per cent of Singaporeans live in HDB estates.

Phil Date Photography

Skyscrapers loom over Chinatown, a tourist and cultural area near Singapore's business district.

But some people wonder if the government moved too fast, destroying irreplaceable fragments of Singapore's heritage as it rushed to build houses and factories. "In the years immediately following independence there was little concern about heritage conservation in Singapore," Asian Studies professor Stephen Dobbs of the University of Western Australia wrote in *The Singapore River.*

"The most important goal was rapid economic development and the building of infrastructure, housing, and amenities to improve the well being of the population through full employment and better living standards," he wrote. "Historical conservation areas such as China-town or stretches of the Singapore River did not enter the planners' minds until the mid-1970s."

Cherian George, a writer and professor at Nanyang Technological University, grew up in Singapore. His childhood home was razed to make room for a highway.

"It's sad that I can't point to a place and say, 'well, yes, this is where I grew up,' because it's gone," George told Discovery Channel while walking through vegetation under an overpass. "But it's nothing different from what most Singaporeans go through. The memory of Singaporeans' childhoods is something that tends to be sacrificed in the name of progress."

193

Chapter 10

POLITICAL EVOLUTION

196

The 1970s was a grand decade for Singapore. Economic output jumped almost fivefold from S$5.8 billion in 1970 to S$25.1 billion in 1980 (adjusted for inflation). Per capita income showed similar stellar growth. And the population grew from about 2 million to 2.4 million.

The price for these economic and social gains was compliance; the mantra from the government: Don't rock the boat. And for a population that remembered the rundown kampongs, the swamps, the Japanese occupation, and the yoke of colonialism, Singapore's independence, growth and progress was a personal story and the price—censored media and a single dominant political party, for instance—was arguably cheap.

"The challenge for Singapore always is how you maintain stability because if you lose stability in Singapore you lose everything," said Kishore Mahbubani, former ambassador to the United Nations from Singapore. "If you live in America, it's like sailing across the ocean in an aircraft carrier. You can jump up and down, and the aircraft carrier's not going to shake. But if you live in Singapore, it's like sailing in a sort of small canoe. If you want to jump up and down in the canoe, the canoe will sink."

Preceding page: Opening of Singapore Legislative Council Meeting

"It was a night that had to be lived to be remembered. And I lived that night. It was wonderful. The crowd just went wild. There was a great feeling that things were perhaps going to change"
— J B Jeyaretnam, secretary general, Workers' Party

But in the beginning of the 1980s, someone rocked the boat. Voters in the Anson district in central Singapore broke the PAP's monopoly in parliament. On 31 October 1981, Joshua Benjamin "JB" Jeyaretnam, a firebrand lawyer and leader of the Worker's Party, won a by-election and claimed a seat in parliament, the first not held by the PAP in 16 year of independence. Though the PAP retained unquestioned control of government, the victory was extraordinary for Singapore.

"It was a night that had to be lived to be remembered. And I lived that night" Jeyaretnam told Discovery Channel years later. "It was wonderful. The crowd just went wild. There was a great feeling that things were perhaps going to change."

197

Jeyaretnam had been rocking the boat since he joined and revived the Workers Party in 1971, but this is the first time he made a splash. He had run for the Anson seat several times, and in 1980 was narrowly defeated by the PAP candidate. He won the by-election in 1981 with 52 per cent of the vote.

Jeyaretnam was seen as a champion of the poorest in Singapore—those who had benefited least from the country's economic success. Though he had won a seat in parliament, he faced a long hard road; the ruling party would not make it easy for him.

Jeyaretnam championed the poor and argued for the sort of welfare system that the PAP opposed.

"We regarded him as rather destructive. He was actually more for welfare, which we were dead against. You offer welfare to the people over two elections, and the place would be destroyed," said Goh Chok Tong.

"I was a bit intimidated, but one gets used to it. You get braver. I was referred no less than six times for unprofessional conduct. And they said that was a record."

– J B Jeyaretnam, secretary general, Workers' Party

Jeyaretnam continued to enjoy widespread support, and in the general election of 1984 he scored another spectacular victory in Anson.

In 1986, however, he was prosecuted over a false declaration of accounts by his Workers' Party. He was acquitted on all but one of the charges, a ruling which the prosecution appealed. Following a retrial ordered by the chief justice, Jeyaretnam was found guilty on all charges. He was jailed for one month, fined $S5,000 and disbarred.

Jeyaretnam appealed the debarment to the Privy Council in London, which upheld his appeal, finding that he had "suffered a grievous injustice". He was reinstated as an attorney, but his criminal conviction remained. Since Singapore was a commonwealth member, the Privy Council could hear certain appeals. Following the decision on the Jeyaretnam case, Singapore closed this avenue of redress.

Jeyaretnam eventually returned to Parliament, though his career was dogged by a series of complex lawsuits brought against him by PAP leaders, including Lee Kuan Yew, who twice successfully sued Jeyaretnam for libel.

"This government has been so long in power they can really believe they are the best government for Singapore, now and in perpetuity," said local author and political commentator Catherine Lim. "I'm almost sure that they want to be a permanent government, not for self glory, but for the good of the country."

And for more than four decades, the PAP has been in control of government, winning general elections with 60 per cent of the vote or more and always holding all but a few parliamentary seats. Unlike Barisan Sosialis members in the 1960s, Singapore's modern political opposition leaders were more likely to be sued for libel, often forcing them into bankruptcy and making them ineligible for office, than jailed indefinitely.

Jeyaretnam's false accounts conviction brought with it a ban from holding office for five years, but he was back in the running in 1997, when he and a party colleague narrowly lost a seat in the Chen San district to the PAP. But for his efforts, Jeyaretnam received a consolation prize, a seat as a non-constituency member of parliament. These seats were given to the opposition party that had the strongest election showing, yet still lost. Non-constituency members are barred from voting on constitutional amendments, public funding bills, no-confidence resolutions against the government, or resolutions to remove the president from office.

The maverick politician with his trademark sideburns was soon brought to court in a series of defamation lawsuits filed by the PAP based on comments during an election rally when he mentioned his fellow Workers Party candidate, Tang Liang Hong, had filed police reports against PAP leaders. Jeyaretnam lost the case, and declared bankruptcy in 2001 when he couldn't pay the damages that had been handed down by the court. The bankruptcy again meant that he was banned from politics until his debt was cleared.

"Jeyaretnam was all sound and fury," Lee wrote in his memoirs. "He made wild allegations of police high-handedness and repeated every grievance disgruntled people channelled through him without checking the facts. That he had no principled stand suited us; he was unlikely to become a credible alternative."

Lee told Discovery Channel that if Jeyaretnam did things that were "out of bounds," he would "pin him down," which the opposition politician later said was phrasing more appropriate for demagogues than democrats.

199

"Jeyaretnam was all sound and fury."
  – Lee Kuan Yew, first prime minister of Singapore

"We are not going to give up that easily, to anybody who would challenge our rule. So we therefore take opposition seriously. When you lose one seat, there is great consternation."

– Goh Chok Tong, prime minister, 1990–2004

In 2008, though, Jeyaretnam was back on the political scene with his newly formed Reform Party, declaring, at 82 years of age, "We are just beginning." Jeyaretnam estimated that he paid out more than S$1.5 million in damages and costs from the many lawsuits he faced. He died in September that year of a heart attack. "Lee Kuan Yew may have been infinitely the greater statesman," The Economist magazine said in an obituary, "but some would have judged Mr. Jeyaretnam the bigger man."

Jeyaretnam was one of a small handful of Singaporeans who raised the voice of opposition in the prosperous city-state. Tang, who was Jeyaretnam's ally on the 1997 elections, was sued for defamation by PAP leaders for saying they had lied in characterizing him as anti-Christian. Tang fled to Malaysia then Australia soon after the election, but he, his family and assets were dogged by the litigation. Chee Soon Juan, who took charge of the Singapore Democratic Party in the late 1990s, was also the target of defamation lawsuits and other charges that generally kept him from running for office and brought him to bankruptcy in 2006.

While the PAP has been criticized for using libel and defamation charges to silence opponents and stifle the media, the party sees it another way. "There are groups who think that we should not have libel actions and that opposition politicians should be given a free run," Lee said during a state visit to London in 1997, "but we who look after Singapore believe that we should uphold and protect the reputation of ministers. ... We believe in keeping up a reputation that is unchallengeable, and if you challenge that reputation and you can't prove in court the truth of what you have said, you pay damages."

J B JEYARETNAM

The man who crashed the PAP's party in Parliament, Joshua Benjamin Jeyaretnam, was born in Sri Lanka in 1926. His parents, who lived in Muar in northern Johor, were visiting their native village, Chankanai, at the time. The family returned to Muar soon after the birth.

Known later by his initials, "JB," Jeyaretnam had a middle-class upbringing. His father was a chief clerk in the Public Works Department in Johore. While the family spoke English at home,

201

Opposition politician Joshua Jeyaretnam smiles during a press conference in his office in Singapore, 16 August 2001. Jeyaretnam defiantly vowed to remain politically active despite losing his parliamentary seat and going bankrupt after fighting the ruling People's Action Party (PAP) for two decades.

the young Jeyaretnam learned Tamil as a second language in the Catholic school in Muar. Jeyaretnam was raised a Christian and went regularly to the local Methodist Episcopal Church of America, a revivalist church with roots in the Church of England.

Jeyaretnam studied Law at University College London and returned to Singapore in 1952 to join the legal service. He rose quickly in the legal establishment, serving as a magistrate, district judge, prosecuting counsel, registrar of the Supreme Court and chief of the Subordinate Judiciary. In 1963 at the age of 37 he resigned and went into private practice. "I was disillusioned, completely," he said.

Jeyaretnam, then spent nearly 10 years in private practice, engaging in politics indirectly as an advisor to churches and other associations. His legal business over at the time was a mixture of conventional criminal cases and civil work, but he also took on a large number of clients whose cases had a political aspect.

In 1971, he was invited to become secretary-general of the Workers' Party, which had been founded by David Marshall a decade earlier. He accepted, a move that proved to be detrimental to his career as a private lawyer. Clients who thought it best to avoid doing business with a politician who was known to be out of favour with the government started moving their business away.

Jeyaretnam spent the next 10 years building the Workers' Party and during that time made five unsuccessful attempts to enter Parliament. Finally, in 1981, he won a seat as member of Parliament for the Anson constituency.

PASSING THE BATON

As the city-state approached the turn of the century, its political evolution continued. In 1990, 31 years after self-rule, modern Singapore would experience for the first time government without Lee Kuan Yew officially at the helm.

Goh Chok Tong, a PAP loyalist, succeeded Lee as prime minister 28 November 1990. As senior minister, a newly created cabinet post, Lee would remain an influential member of the government and quickly don the mantle of respected elder statesman in Asia. Talking with Discovery Channel later, Goh said, "My own mission when I took over was: How do I keep Singapore going? I am not Lee Kuan Yew. I can't govern like him. I did not fight for independence. I took over Singapore, in a sense, with everything in good working order."

What Goh promised Singapore was a kinder, gentler society, and a more open political culture. During his mandate, opposition politicians were no longer such a rarity, although they still accounted for a small fraction of the seats in parliament. While elsewhere in Asia, long-standing governments had begun to topple, Singapore's PAP never won less than 60 per cent of the popular vote in general elections.

203

"The ties between the elected leaders and the people...must be constantly nurtured through continual discussion, feedback and explanation" so that the government *"will have a close feel of the mood of the people, and the people will understand thoroughly what is at stake and what needs to be done"*

– Goh Chok Tong, prime minister, 1990–2004

GOH CHOK TONG

Goh Chok Tong, born in Singapore during the Japanese occupation, came from a humble background. His family shared a house with several other families. His father died when Goh was still young, and Goh and his sister were raised by their mother, their grandmother, and their uncle and aunt. Goh's mother worked as a teacher.

Singapore Press Holdingss

Goh Chok Tong became prime minister of Singapore when Lee Kuan Yew stepped down in 1990.

Like Lee Kuan Yew, Goh was educated at Raffles Institution, where he excelled not just academically, but also in sports. Goh was an active student—a scout, captain of the swim team, editor of the school magazine and vice-head prefect. He was interested in writing and was described by his schoolmates as a good writer. At the 30th anniversary reunion dinner of the Raffles Institution Class of 1958, Goh confessed that he had become a politician by default. He had in his youth always aspired to be a journalist. He went on to the University of Singapore in 1961 to study economics. In 1964 Goh finished top in a class of 19 students, obtaining a First Class Honours degree in economics.

Upon graduation, he joined the Singapore Civil Service (SCS) as an administrative officer. In 1966, he won a fellowship to Williams College in the United States and completed the MA programme in Development Economics.

In 1965, at age 24, Goh married Tan Choo Leng, an advocate and solicitor. Four years later, they became the parents of twins.

Goh returned to his job in the SCS and worked as an economic planner and research economist after graduating from Williams College. In August 1969, he was seconded to Neptune Orient Lines Ltd (NOL), a newly incorporated government company and Singapore's national shipping line, as planning and projects manager. He went on to take a permanent position within NOL and enjoyed a meteoric rise up the corporate ladder. He was appointed financial controller and later financial director on the NOL board of directors. After only four years in the company, Goh was appointed managing director. It was his success at NOL, turning it into a profitable enterprise for the first time. His success caught the attention of then Finance Minister Hon Sui Sen, who persuaded Goh to enter politics.

Goh followed Hon's suggestion. He left NOL and stood in the December 1976 general election as PAP candidate for the Marine Parade constituency. He won the seat with a convincing majority of 10,496 votes, 76.8 per cent of the vote. Throughout the next 15 years, he took on various portfolios, including finance, trade and industry, defence, and health. He was appointed senior minister of state at the ministry of finance in September 1977. He held that post until March 1979, when he was promoted to the position of minister for trade and industry. In January 1981 he was given the additional portfolio of health. As the minister for health in 1981, Goh introduced the Medisave scheme, which enabled Singaporeans to use their Central Provident Fund to pay medical bills. He became first deputy prime minister in 1985 and prime minister in November 1990. He won three general elections as prime minister. Under Goh, the PAP saw its share of the vote increase by four percentage points to 65 per cent in 1997, and then to 75 per cent in 2001.

206

"They've (Singaporeans) experienced the most dramatic increase in standard of living that any people have experienced probably ever since the beginning of man. And then you ask these people: why aren't you revolting? Why aren't you going out in the streets? But why should they?"

– Kishore Mahbubani, former UN Ambassador

The PAP's heavy-handed way of dealing with its opposition has been criticised, yet its style of government has survived, and indeed thrived, for many years.

In 1993, Singapore's political and legal system came under the global media spotlight when Michael Fay, an American teenager then living in Singapore, was convicted of vandalism and theft. He was given a S$3,500 fine, and sentenced to four months in prison and six lashes of the cane.

Corporal punishment in the Singapore penal system is administered with a rattan cane. Each stroke of the cane splits the skin and after three lashes, victims can go into shock.

The sentencing of Fay drew global attention, and also the attention of then US President Bill Clinton, who noted that Fay, "is going to bleed considerably and may have permanent scars", and said he believed the punishment was a mistake.

Prime Minister Goh Chok Tong responded: "Why should there be a law for Americans and a different law for Singaporeans? I thought Americans believed in the rule of law."

207

The Michael Fay incident drew considerable media attention to Singapore. Some US media denounced Singapore as a "dictatorship", "a repressive place", and a "lawless state", and called the caning "torture". Some lobbyists called for Americans to stop visiting Singapore or to stop using its national airline, and for American companies to stop investing and doing business in the country. The caning sentence became an international human rights issue.

"I myself had difficulty making an appointment to see President Clinton in the first two years (of my term). The White House aides did not put the request of Singapore up to the President. But in the longer term it was good for us, because Singapore was prepared to stand up against mighty America."

– Goh Chok Tong, prime minister, 1990 – 2004

AFP

*US student Michael Fay (left) arrives at the High Court
with his stepfather Marco Chan (centre), 31 March 1994.
Fay, 18, was appealing his sentence of four months in jail
and six strokes from a cane on two counts of vandalism.*

The sentence was reduced from six strokes to four as a gesture to President Clinton. Noting that Clinton had appealed privately for clemency and had commented on the case publicly three times, the government said in a statement that, "to reject his appeal totally would show an unhelpful disregard for the president and the domestic pressures on him on this issue." It added that "the government values Singapore's good relations with the United States and the constructive economic and security role of the United States in the region."

Goh added later, "In the longer term it was good for us that Singapore was prepared to stand up to America."

Fay, sentenced to four months in prison along with his caning, was released from Singapore's Queensland Remand Centre on 21 June 1995. He received time off for good behaviour and served just 83 days of his term. He returned to the United States the next day. For months after his repatriation, Singapore media followed his every public misdeed, from coming home drunk and "scuffling" with his father to minor injuries suffered while working on a car to burning his face while sniffing butane and entering rehab.

Back in America, Fay appeared on several television shows and the possibility of a book or film describing his experience was mooted, but this did not materialise. Fay claimed that he was innocent of the charges he was sentenced for, that he had not vandalised any car and had simply taken some traffic signs. He said he had confessed under torture.

As a result of the Michael Fay incident, some foreign media developed a fascination for a country that seemed so Western on the surface, but had such a different approach to social control. The ban on the sale or use of chewing gum attracted attention, as did the deployment of undercover environmental health officers to ensure that people using public lavatories flush afterwards.

"They've experienced the most dramatic increase in standard of living that any people have ever experienced, probably since the beginning of man," Mahbubani said of his countrymen. "And then you ask these people, 'Why aren't you revolting? Why aren't you going out in the streets?' Well, why should they?"

209

NICK LEESON

A second crime in the 1990s would keep the world's attention on the small city-state in Southeast Asia— this one far more spectacular with effects that were felt worldwide. Nick Leeson, the 28-year-old head of Barings Bank's futures trading in Singapore, amassed losses through unauthorized trades that grew to $1.4 billion and eventually brought the collapse of the venerable Barings Bank.

A native of Watford just outside London, Leeson came to Singapore in 1992 to set up and run Barings' futures trading on the Singapore Stock Exchange. With a purported salary of £50,000 a year, plus annual bonuses of almost three times that amount, Leeson raked in large profits for the bank in derivatives trading, a relatively new financial market that few understood completely. But when Leeson began making losses, he hid the losses in an account the bank used to correct errors made on trades.

Leeson focused on Nikkei 225 stock index, placing large bets in hopes of covering previous losses. But when Asian markets plunged following the 1995 earthquake in Kobe, the losses soon became too great to conceal. Leeson left a handwritten note, "I'm sorry," on his desk and fled with his wife to Malaysia on 27 February 1995, setting off a global manhunt.

Barings was founded in 1762 and in 1995 was Britain's oldest merchant bank. It counted Queen Elizabeth among its clients.

Associated Press

Rogue trader Nick Leeson is escorted through Frankfurt Airport following his arrest, 1995.

210

But the $1.4 billion in losses Leeson left was twice the bank's available trading capital. The losses kept mounting, and within a week after Leeson's flight they reached $2.2 billion. After a failed bailout attempt by the Bank of England, Barings collapsed on 27 February 1995.

Known in headlines as the "rogue trader," Leeson enjoyed a few more days of freedom before being arrested on 2 March 1995 in Frankfurt's airport following a flight from Brunei. Nine months later, he was extradited to Singapore, where he pleaded guilty to two charges of fraud and forgery and was sentenced to 6½ years in prison. He was released in July 1999, early for good behaviour.

Since his release, Leeson has published two books, became a regular on the speaking circuit, and eventually became CEO of the Galway United Football Club in Ireland. His first book, *Rogue Trader*, was made into a movie in 1999 with Ewan McGregor in the title role.

MILESTONES IN SINGAPORE'S LEGAL HISTORY

THE FIRST CHARTER OF JUSTICE

Singapore's First Charter of Justice was incorporated in the treaty signed by Sir Thomas Stamford Raffles, Sultan Hussein of Johor and Temenggong Abdul Rahman on 6 February 1819. In 1807, the Crown had granted the East India Company a Charter of Justice which allowed it to establish a Court in Penang.

THE SECOND CHARTER OF JUSTICE

The Second Charter of Justice was issued on 27 November 1826. This Charter abolished the Recorder's Court and established the Court of Judicature of Prince of Wales' Island (Penang), Singapore and Malaya. In criminal proceedings, the court was to administer criminal justice in such "manner and form" as the courts in Britain, with "due attention being (given) to the several religions, manners and usages of the native Inhabitants". The governor and the resident Councillor acted as two judges of the court. The third judge was the recorder, who was based on Penang and had to travel on circuit to Malacca and Singapore from his home base.

THE THIRD CHARTER OF JUSTICE

The Third Charter of Justice of 12 August 1855 was granted to cope with the increase in the judicial workload that had resulted from Singapore's rapid development. Under the Third Charter of Justice, the Court of Judicature was reorganised into two divisions. The first division had jurisdiction over Singapore and Malacca and comprised the recorder of Singapore, the governor and the resident councillors of Singapore and Malacca. The second division had jurisdiction over Prince of Wales' Island and Province Wellesley, and comprised the recorder of Prince of Wales' Island, the governor and the resident councillor of Prince of Wales' Island.

THE JUDICIAL SYSTEM: 1868 - 1941

The Judicial Duties Act of 1867 brought about further changes to Singapore's judicial system. The governor of the Straits Settlements ceased to be a judge of the Court of Judicature, although the resident councillors continued to sit under their new title of lieutenant-governors. The Supreme Court Ordinance 1868 abolished the Court of Judicature of Prince of Wales' Island, Singapore and Malacca, replacing it with the Supreme Court of the Straits Settlements. In turn, the Courts Ordinance of 1873 reconstituted the court, so that it now consisted of the chief justice, the judge of Penang, a senior and a junior puisne judge. One division of the court sat in Singapore and Malacca, while another sat in Penang.

THE JAPANESE OCCUPATION

Singapore's courts were shuttered when the Japanese invaded in 1942 and established a Military Court of Justice to administer military ordinances and the laws of the Japanese army. The courts were re-opened by a proclamation dated 27 May 1942, which stated that they were to follow the former legal system insofar as it did not interfere with the military administration. The Syonan Supreme Court or "Syonan Koto-Hoin" was opened on 29 May 1942. A court of appeal was also created but never sat.

THE POST-WAR YEARS

Following the surrender of the Japanese on 12 September 1945, Singapore was temporarily administered by the British Military Administration, which proclaimed that all Japanese proclamations and decrees ceased to have effect, and that "all laws and customs existing immediately prior to the Japanese occupation will be respected". The British Military Administration came to an end on 31 March 1946, when the Supreme Court, consisting of a High Court and a Court of Appeal, was constituted by the Singapore Colony Order in Council. The Court of Criminal Appeal continued to function. Final appeals lay with the Judicial Committee of the Privy Council in London.

POST-INDEPENDENCE

Although Singapore became independent on 9 August 1965, ties between the judicial systems of Singapore and Malaysia were not severed until 1969. The Supreme Court of Judicature Act 1969, re-established the Supreme Court of Singapore, comprising the High Court, the Court of Appeal and the Court of Criminal Appeal. Jury trials were abolished in 1969, by an amendment to the Criminal Procedure Code, which provided for trials of capital offences to be heard by two judges. This arrangement continued until 18 April 1992, when the Criminal Procedure Code was amended to allow trials of capital offences to be heard before a single Judge.

The next important milestone for Singapore's judicial system was the introduction of judicial commissioners to the Supreme Court Bench. A judicial commissioner is appointed for specific periods of time and may exercise the powers and perform the functions of a judge. In this capacity, a commissioner enjoys the same immunities as a judge. In 1993, the existing appellate court, which comprised the Court of Appeal and the Court of Criminal Appeal, was reconstituted into a single Court of Appeal for both civil and criminal appeals. The present Court of Appeal comprises the chief justice and the judges of appeal, who rank above high court judges. A judge of the High Court may also, on the request of the chief justice, sit as a judge of the Court of Appeal.

213

214

AFP

Former Prime Minister Goh Chok Tong (left) shakes hands with newly installed
Prime Minister Lee Hsien Loong (centre) as President S.R. Nathan (right) looks on after the
oath taking ceremony at the Istana presidential palace in Singapore, 12 August 2004.

Goh saw Singapore through several challenging events. The Asian financial crisis in 1997 was one. During this time, many countries in the region saw slumping currencies, devalued stock markets and a spectacular rise in private debt. Although Singapore suffered serious dips in the stock and property markets, its economy weathered the storm, and by 1999 the economy had rebounded strongly. Singapore's resilience was attributed to the government's skilful response to the regional turmoil and its active and effective management of the resulting recession. This resilience also carried the economy through the collapse of the dot.com bubble in 2000 and the climate of global tension created by the 9/11 terrorist attacks in 2001.

In late 2001, Goh's government had to deal with terrorism in its own backyard. A series of Jemaah Islamiah (JI) bomb plots was uncovered in Singapore. The Southeast Asian terrorist group was planning to attack a range of targets, including western interests and local installations. Some 31 persons were detained in two security operations against the JI group between 2002 and 2003. In 2004, restrictive orders under the Internal Security Act (ISA) were issued against 12 persons. In August 2004, a National Security Strategy was developed to counter this threat.

Not the least of the challenges faced by the country during Goh's tenure was the outbreak of SARS in 2003. Singapore's handling of the crisis was highly praised by the World Health Organisation. Singapore, for example, used its tight control on society to impose home quarantines and jail those in violation. The government also embarked on a communications strategy spearheaded by Goh that didn't dismiss people's fears and offered practical advice on staying healthy. One observer, risk expert Peter Sandman, wrote that Singapore's strategy amounted to "harnessing the public's fear instead of trying to squelch it" The government also managed to limit the economic impact of SARS; despite the outbreak, the country's economy saw growth of 2.9 per cent that year.

In August 2004, after 14 years as prime minister, Goh stepped aside and Lee Kuan Yew's eldest son Lee Hsien Loong became the country's third prime minister. Goh moved into the role of senior minister, while the senior Lee was named minister mentor, continuing his role as elder statesman.

Lee Hsien Loong would be leading Singapore through a much different world than his father faced when he first became prime minister 45 years earlier. Advances in communications—whether travel opportunities, scores of channels available on cable television, or the internet—have made it much more difficult to isolate Singaporeans from political currents in the rest of the world. The low-hanging fruit of economic development had been harvested. And three years into his term, he faced the greatest global recession since the Great Depression almost a century earlier.

"Singapore is now at another major transition point," Lee told the Harvard Club of Singapore a few months before being sworn in as prime minister. "It is not just a changing of the guard. Our world has changed irrevocably. A younger generation born after independence is now in majority, and our strategies to grow our economy and root our people must change."

He said the government must continue to progressively "widen the limits of openness" because the world is more uncertain and Singaporeans are better educated and more informed. The young generation needs room to make mistakes and experiment.

"If we want a more participatory citizenry, the government will have to cut the apron strings and leave more matters to the private and people sectors," he said. "Nanny should not look after everything all the time."

Perhaps the most visible signs of the new Singapore are the two hotel-casino projects, one rising on the outskirts of the central business district and the other on the Sentosa tourist island. Both were scheduled to open in 2010, after delays brought by the global economic crisis. Lee announced plans to build integrated resorts, as they are known in Singapore, in late 2004. The news sparked an unusually raucous debate, played out in the readers' comments section of the *Straits Times* and elsewhere. Although voices opposing the plan were loud, the government said in April 2005 that it would go ahead with the initiative. Measures would be taken to limit problems locally, such as increased help for problem gamblers and entrance fees to the casinos for citizens and foreigners registered as permanent residents.

Getty Images

Lee Kuan Yew (left) receives his credentials as minister mentor from his son, Lee Hsien Loong, the country's third prime minister, 2004.

LEE HSIEN LOONG

In the Chinese calendar, 10 February 1952 was an auspicious date, the 15th day of the first moon of the year of the dragon, Lee Kuan Yew recounted in his memoirs. So, consulting a Supreme Court interpreter for an appropriate name for a son born on that date, he chose Hsien Loong, "illustrious dragon."

Lee Hsien Loong was born in Singapore. He studied at Nanyang Primary School and National Junior College. (Also in his memoirs, the senior Lee noted that the Chinese press carried pictures of his son at Nanyang Kindergarten, which taught in Chinese. "My determination that my three children should be educated in the language and culture of their ancestors gave me credentials that the communists could never impugn," he wrote.) Lee Hsien Loong obtained a degree in mathematics and a diploma in computer science at Cambridge University, and went on for a master's in public administration at Harvard University's Kennedy School of Government.

Lee enlisted in the Singapore armed forced in 1971, rising to the rank of brigadier general by 1978. He left the military and entered politics, winning a parliamentary seat from the Teck Ghee district in 1984. Two years later he was elected to the Central Executive Committee of the PAP. He became minister of trade and industry in 1987.

In 1990, Lee was appointed deputy prime minister in Goh's cabinet with a focus on the economy and civil service. While holding this position, he was also finance minister from 2001 to 2007 and chairman of the Monetary Authority of Singapore (MAS) from 1998 to 2004. As MAS chairman, he steered the country's monetary policy through the brunt of the Asian Financial Crisis, which began in 1997.

As Singapore moved further into the 21st Century, the government has spread its bets widely, covering film, biotechnology, theme parks and many other promising positions in the hope of safeguarding Singapore's economic well-being.

Associated Press

Singapore Prime Minister Lee Hsien Loong (left) welcomes US President Barack Obama to Singapore during an Asia-Pacific Economic Cooperation (APEC) meeting, 2009.

Chapter 11

ENTERING THE 21ST CENTURY

As Singapore entered the 21st Century, the island-state faced a new set of challenges and opportunities. The economic model that had brought prosperity for its first four decades as an independent country—business friendly, talented workers, and low wages—was succumbing to competition from other Asian states, particularly China and India. The model had lost its distinctiveness and ability to drive the country forward. Much like Raffles in the 19th Century and Lee Kuan Yew in the 20th, Singapore's new leaders would have to reinvent their country and their economy. They had to find a way to keep it relevant amid new global economic patterns.

Late in 2009, Senior Minister Goh Chok Tong warned, "Singapore's competitive advantages are fast being eroded as other cities start to acquire similar abilities. Singapore must, therefore, project a new identity, one that captivates the eyes, moves the heart, stirs the soul, and inspires the mind." The senior minister stressed that Singaporeans, foreigners registered as permanent residents and foreign workers all have roles to play. "If Singapore cannot differentiate itself as an outstanding city, we would not be able to sustain our high quality of life," he said.

But could a country built on *laissez-faire* economics and tight social and political controls, embrace innovation, creativity and free thinking fast enough? Can a country often derided as a "nanny state" by foreign media cut the apron strings without risking the island's carefully guarded stability?

Preceding page: Singaporean celebrate after the city-state was announced as the host of the 2010 Youth Olympics, in Singapore on 21 February 2008.

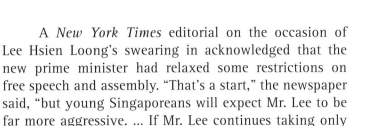

A *New York Times* editorial on the occasion of Lee Hsien Loong's swearing in acknowledged that the new prime minister had relaxed some restrictions on free speech and assembly. "That's a start," the newspaper said, "but young Singaporeans will expect Mr. Lee to be far more aggressive. ... If Mr. Lee continues taking only half-steps toward a more tolerant and democratic society, Singapore's vaunted prosperity will very likely suffer."

To attract higher valued foreign investments, those that rely on innovation rather than skilled repetition of one task, Singapore had to compete with other cities with a far more dynamic reputations. The country began focusing on its arts, food and nightlife, allowing for instance table-top dancing in some bars (but no nudity) and reverse bungee jumping, in which riders are flung into the air strapped in a giant sling shot. Perhaps symbolic, the reverse bungee jumping attraction is set on the site on the Singapore River that Whampoa once used for warehouses.

Author Catherine Lim said that she's astonished that the government has allowed many of these activities. But she observed that the government has done little to relax the PAP's political control.

"In the political domain, they remain adamant and a little bit squeamish about opening up because, I suspect, this is one area that would challenge their entrenched position. The risks are greater there," she said. "You have a situation that some of us who like a little bit of noise, mess, a little bit of even unruliness, might describe as antiseptic, clinical."

223

"I describe it as a kind of uneasy dance, between the government and the people. We allow you three steps forward, but if you are not behaving, we pull you back two steps. I suppose incrementally, there will be an increase in the end, but for a whole lot of Singaporeans, too slowly."

– Catherine Lim, Singapore author

In 2000, the government established a speakers' corner designed to serve as a popular platform for political ideas and opinions. The site reflects the more famous Speakers' Corner in London's Hyde Park, an innovation in free speech from the mid-19th century. Characteristically, the Singapore initiative was accompanied by a list of restrictions. Speakers had to be registered in advance and were forbidden from addressing topics related to race or religion and no amplification is allowed. On the day the Speaker's Corner opened, more than 15 people registered to speak, and there has been a number of events there, in support of different causes. At first, hundreds gathered to hear those speaking, but the corner soon lost its novelty. Soon it was rare for more than a handful of idlers to be present for the few speakers who register.

After independence, Singapore was able to leverage an efficient infrastructure and competitive labour force into decades of sustained and substantial economic growth, but it did not do this in a vacuum. Its success depended on riding the waves of global and regional political, economic and social change. At the start of the new millennium the rise of India and China and the relative decline of Japan and the original tiger economies meant that Singapore had to recalibrate its own policies.

224

Speakers' Corner at Hong Lim Park.

225

Finished in 2008, the Singapore Flyer rises 165 meters high.
When opened it was the world's tallest ferris wheel.

"The world has changed," observed Tony Tan, Singapore's deputy prime minister from 1995 – 2005.

So Singapore has to look ahead, and look elsewhere. Some saw its future in the hands of people like Nickson Fong, an entrepreneur whose entire industry is based on thinking outside the box.

Fong moved from Singapore to America in the 1980s and studied computer animation. Twenty years later he returned to Singapore to make the country's first big budget animated movie. He was presented by the Singapore government as a role model, an entrepreneur who set up a company, Egg Story, in a new, creative industry. In this respect he was seen as being part of the Singapore tradition of rising to new challenges and adapting to new circumstances. But Fong pointed out that it was hard to find other Singaporeans willing to work with him in the open and creative way that the animation field requires— nearly all the animators on his first Singapore project were from elsewhere in Asia.

226

Egg Story

Nickson Fong of Egg Story has been presented as a role model for Singapore.

IMPORTING TALENT

Singapore, limited by its geographical and population size, has always had to seek talent from beyond its shores. In 2000, the Singapore Department of Statistics recorded that—excluding tourists—foreign permanent and non-permanent residents accounted for a quarter of the population. In fact, the jump in the population, to 4.02 million in 2000 from 3.05 million in 1990, was attributed largely to an influx of foreigners. Citizens made up 74 per cent of the population, down from 86 per cent in 1990.

In 1997, Goh launched the Singapore 21 Committee and charged it with strengthening the "heartware" of the country going into the new century. One area of focus was attracting foreign talent, professionals from overseas that would settle at least temporarily in the country.

The committee report in 2000 warned that Singaporeans are afraid that the influx of foreign professionals would crowd them out of the market. "If the inflow of foreign talent leads to its citizens losing their sense of affiliation to this country, Singapore is the poorer, even if in material terms we may be one of the richest in the world," it said, adding that the solution is to explain more clearly why foreign professionals are needed.

"Foreign talent are to Singapore what brooks are to a river: they help to make it stronger and flow faster," the report said. "Many things we take for granted would not have been possible without them. ... Talented foreigners are partners with Singaporeans in our global competition for scarce resources. It is better that they be part of the Singapore team ... than out there on another team competing against Singapore."

In his 2002 National Day Rally speech, Prime Minister Goh Chok Tong, urged Singaporeans to embrace the idea of foreign talent: "We should welcome any international talent who decides to sink roots in Singapore. If they feel enough for Singapore to want to make it their home, let us embrace them warmly. We need to send a clear signal to all those who can raise our standards whether in sports, music, dance, the theatre, literature,

228

*Opened in 2002, Esplanade Theatres on the Bay was purpose built
to be Singapore's centre for performing arts.*

"Foreign talent are to Singapore what brooks are to a river: they help to make it stronger and flow faster."

the economy or politics, that they are welcome. We have become what we are because we have attracted international talent."

He added, "If a huge country like the US has embraced foreign talent, we, with only three million people, must be crazy not to do so. Because of the quality of our people, and our economic success and social progress, we are taken seriously by other countries. We enjoy an influence disproportionate to our size. But if we now shut our doors to talent, we will soon become like any other Third World city of three million people. Then we will find life quite different. We will become a small fish—a guppy—in a small pond. To swim among the big fishes in the ocean, we have to top up our population with international talent."

The outflow of local talent has not helped the situation. Many Singaporeans, lured by the opportunities offered by larger economies, are venturing overseas to work. Yet Singaporeans remain optimistic. Lee Kuan Yew pointed out during an interview in Bahrain in March 2008, "It's a mobile world in which our attractiveness as a society will determine our future. If we are unattractive as a society, economically stagnant or slothful, then we are out of this game of attracting talent. For the time being, we are on top of the game, we are attracting more talent than we are losing."

Singapore is still among the top 10 countries in the region in terms of intellectual property and capital, but maintaining this position will depend on maintaining an ability to attract foreign talent. This, Lee Kuan Yew argued,

230

Attracting foreign talent is the "key to Singapore's future," says Lee Kuan Yew.

is the "key to Singapore's future", since the country's small population means that it cannot produce as much talent as it needs.

Importing talent is also necessary for Singapore to respond to fast-changing economic and technological trends. Developing or training human resources from the ground up takes time whereas importing talent when it is required reduces the time lag—a tactic that Singapore has always used.

In 2007, Singapore's Ministry of Manpower introduced a Personalised Employment Pass (PEP) to "better attract and retain global talent". The PEP is granted to suitable foreigners with employment passes or foreigners who have graduated from Singapore universities, and have worked in the country for a period of time. Unlike the employment pass, which is tied to a specific employer, the PEP is granted on the strength of an EP holder's individual merits and allows the holder to remain in

Singapore for up to six months between jobs to evaluate new employment opportunities. In a statement issued by the ministry it was argued that the new policy would make it possible "to retain selected global talent who would otherwise have to leave Singapore".

The ministry statement pointed out that in the intensified global competition for talent, the PEP would strengthen Singapore's attractiveness to highly skilled foreigners. "This will help grow the overall economic pie in Singapore, creating more jobs and opportunities for Singaporeans," it said.

Among the fields in which Singapore has sought to import talent are banking, finance, information technology, research and development, and higher education. In 2008, more than 5,000 PhDs were working in research and development in Singapore, more than half of whom were foreign citizens.

Another focus was in the sporting arena. In 1993, a Foreign Sports Talent scheme was introduced to accelerate the citizenship process for promising foreign athletes. It was hoped the scheme would raise Singapore's sports profile and that it would also inspire young Singaporeans to follow in the footsteps of naturalised Singaporeans who have excelled at sports.

231

More than 54 foreign-born athletes became Singaporeans in the decade and a half after the introduction of the scheme. Foreign-born athletes accounted for 35 per cent of Singapore's 43 gold medals at the 2007 SEA Games in Thailand, though they made up just 7.6 per cent of the 423-strong Singapore contingent. However,

"It's a mobile world in which our attractiveness as a society will determine our future. If we are unattractive as a society, economically stagnant or slothful, then we are out of this game of attracting talent."
– Lee Kuan Yew, first prime minister of Singapore

there was also a high drop-out rate, with some athletes choosing to return to their native countries after competing for Singapore.

A case-in-point involved the Singapore Athletic Association's decision to bring eight China-born athletes to Singapore and sponsor their naturalisation. The exercise cost around S$1 million in public funds, but although three of the athletes eventually became Singapore citizens, only thrower Zhang Guirong continued in active training. Throwers Du Xianhui and Zhang Guirong were reported to have had a stormy relationship with the Athletic Association. Du returned to China. Another shot putter, Dong Enxin, disappeared in late 2007 after costing the Athletic Association around S$288,000 in living and competition expenses while in Singapore. However, he did win a SEA Games gold medal, in 2003.

Concerns were also raised over the emphasis on importing foreign talent, which was viewed by some as necessarily resulting in a downgrading of efforts to groom young local talent. The sports bodies responsible for table tennis and badminton were both accused of neglecting the development of local talent. Half of the 10-member Singapore badminton team that finished a best-ever third in the team event at the 2007 World Junior Championships were foreign-born. The Singapore Women's table tennis team won a silver medal at the 2008 Beijing Summer Olympics. All three players originally hail from China. The medal in Beijing was Singapore's first Olympic medal since 1960 when Tan Howe Liang won a silver medal in men's lightweight weight-lifting.

AFP/Getty Images

Singapore's Olympic table-tennis team is largely made up of athletes who have come from other countries.

LUCASFILM ANIMATION IN SINGAPORE

In August 2004, George Lucas' Lucasfilm Ltd announced it would establish a digital animation studio in Singapore.

Lucasfilm Animation Singapore produces digital animated content, including films, television programmes and games for global audiences.

"I've been a fan of Asian animation and illustration all my life. Asian cinema has had a particularly big impact on a lot of my work. When we began thinking about developing new ways to explore the craft of animation, it seemed a natural step to combine the two," Lucas said. "By having a base in Singapore, we can create a new style of animation that will blend East and West and offer something not seen before."

Announcing the launch of the venture, Micheline Chau, president and chief operating officer of Lucasfilm Ltd, said Singapore was chosen for its "growing talent base, cosmopolitan flavour, and attractiveness as a place to live."

234

Singapore Press Holdings

Lucas General Manager Christian Kubsch with the venerable Yoda.

"By having a base in Singapore, we can create a new style of animation that will blend East and West and offer something not seen before."

– George Lucas, film director

"Young people must read beyond the text book. They must see beyond a scene in a movie."
– Philip Yeo, chairman, Economic Development Board 1986-2001

Added Teo Ming Kian, chairman of the EDB, "This is a capstone for Singapore's digital media industry. We already have an established base of 17 international cable and satellite broadcasters, a burgeoning TV production sector as well as games development. This new studio will not only provide exceptional career opportunities for local animators and people keen in the creative arts, it will also attract top talent from the world over to live and work in Singapore. It will help us further diversify our economy and provide opportunities for our people with different interests and competencies."

To nurture more flexible and inquiring minds, the government has targeted the education system for a complete overhaul. The object is to ensure that the next generations of Singaporeans will be able to think outside the box.

The government also sees Singapore's future in new areas such as biotechnology. It has invested half a billion Singapore dollars in the Biopolis project, an elaborate biotechnology centre. While most of the staff are foreigners, the government believes that the next generation of Singaporeans will be able to learn the new ways of working that are required by centres such as this. It wants Singaporeans to rely on ingenuity as well as hard work.

235

SINGAPORE'S BIOPOLIS

Singapore's Biopolis, launched in October 2003, was conceived as the cornerstone of a much broader vision to build up the biomedical sciences industry in the country. Officiating at the launch, Deputy Prime Minister Tony Tan said the biomedical sciences industry would generate economic wealth for Singapore, create jobs, and improve the health of the population and the quality of life.

Another of the Biopolis' principal objectives, Tan said, was to attract top talent to undertake world-class research in Singapore.

Developed by the government at a cost of S$500 million, Phase 1 of Biopolis comprises a seven-building complex linked by sky bridges, and offers a built-up area of 185,000 sqm. Two buildings are dedicated to biomedical players from the private sector. The other five house the biomedical research institutes of the Agency of Science, Technology and Research, Singapore's lead agency for scientific research and development. The five research institutes are the BioInformatics Institute, the Bioprocessing Technology Institute, the Genome Institute of Singapore, the Institute of Molecular and Cell Biology and the Institute of Bioengineering & Nanotechnology. A fully occupied Biopolis in Phase 1 is expected to be home to 2,000 scientists.

The Biopolis is part of a master plan for a much larger 200-hectare development known as "one-north" and there are provisions for expansion to cater to a growing demand from biotech companies.

Outdoor sculpture at the Biopolis, Singapore's hub for bio-technology research.

AFP/Getty Images

One of the Biopolis' principal objectives is to attract world-class research to Singapore.

REINVENTING SINGAPORE

In 2003, the Singapore government led by then prime minister Goh Chok Tong, announced the launch of the "Remaking Singapore" committee to look at various aspects—economic, social, cultural and political—of change that would take Singapore through the next chapter of its history.

Said Goh at an event to announce the committee's recommendations, "Singapore is now facing one of the most critical periods in our history. Our economic relevance is being tested. The terrorist threat has put pressure on our social cohesion. And Singaporeans are wondering what part they have in the future of this country. The challenges we face are many, and complex. To understand and address them well, we need to look at the problems from many perspectives."

On the social front, Goh explained why Singapore had to reinvent itself. He said it no longer made sense, at this stage in the country's development, "for the government to always control and regulate every activity", adding that "there comes a point where you must take the risk and let go, in order for your child to grow and learn."

To illustrate how Singapore could do this, Goh pointed to an unusual example. "Take bungee jumping. It is not an activity that I would do. But I accept that some of you may want a rush of adrenaline from jumping off a high bridge, suspended from a rope. So we will now allow bungee jumping in Singapore. In fact, so changed is our mindset that we will even allow reverse bungee jumping, which shoots you upwards into the sky."

Aiming for the sky was an apt metaphor for Singapore's optimistic and creative approach to its future. In reinventing itself so as to remain an attractive environment for local-born and foreign-born citizens, Singapore reviewed the quality and role of one of its most iconic thoroughfares—Orchard Road.

239

"There comes a point where you must take the risk and let go, in order for your child to grow and learn."

– Goh Chok Tong, prime minister, 1990-2004

ORCHARD ROAD

In October 2007, the Singapore Tourism Board announced plans for a S$40 million makeover of Singapore's premier shopping belt, Orchard Road. More than seven million tourists visit Orchard Road annually, making it Singapore's most popular attraction. The makeover would introduce new plants and flowers, as well as new street furniture and state-of-the-art lighting. Orchard Road would be divided into three sections: fruit, flower and forest. This would make the pedestrian mall more attractive and create space for arts and cultural events. Other plans included the sale of vacant sites for new malls and wooing more exciting retail concepts to the district.

In 2008 and 2009 three new shopping and entertainment centres—ION Orchard, 313 at Somerset and Orchard Central—were added to Orchard Road's array of retail and leisure outlets.

"Amid a rapidly changing global landscape, Orchard Road needs to go one notch up in order to boost its standing as Singapore's prime shopping and lifestyle hub," said Margaret Teo, assistant chief executive (Leisure) of the Singapore Tourism Board.

As part of the effort to rid itself of its "stuffy" image, Singapore also announced that it would begin allowing casinos to operate in the country. It had already made considerable progress in turning itself into a global arts centre and had begun to show up regularly in global surveys of the most desirable places to live. In July 2008 the prestigious global affairs magazine, *Monocle*, placed Singapore alongside cities such as Sydney, Paris and Barcelona in its ranking of the world's most "alluring" urban centres.

By Courtesy of ION Orchard

The Orchard Road shopping belt will be spruced up in a makeover worth S$40 million to enhance its appeal to visitors.

EVENTS CITY

As part of Singapore's extreme makeover, the government made a push to attract top shelf special events. One of the most prominent—and loudest—is Formula One motor racing. The first Singapore Grand Prix was staged in September 2008 with the domestic telephone service SingTel the major sponsor. The race was the first Formula One grand prix held at night. The street circuit focused on the city's Marina Bay area and passed many of the city's architectural landmarks.

Negotiation for the race began in 2007, with Formula One officials stressing the need to the race to be held at night in order to accommodate the European television audience. Lighting the circuit required almost 1600 floodlights and more than 100 kilometre of cabling. Singapore gained the rights to stage the race for five years, with the possibility of extending the agreement for another five.

242

The first run was won by Fernando Alonso for Renault, but the Formula One governing body, Fédération Internationale de l'Automobile, later ruled that Alonso's teammate had purposely crashed during the race to give Renault an edge. An estimated 300,000 people attended the three-day event. The second Singapore Grand Prix was held in 2009, and the winner was Lewis Hamilton, driving for McLaren-Mercedes. Attendance was estimated at 240,000, with the drop from the previous year blamed on the economic downturn. The television audience for both events was estimated at about 100 million viewers.

"I am very pleased to welcome Singapore to the Formula One family and we look forward to this exotic addition to the championship... this will be first fully lit street race in Formula One."
– Bernie Ecclestone, CEO of Formula One Management

Singapore staged the first Formula One Grand Prix in 2008 night race.

Singapore also went after A-list international athletic events. In February 2008, the country was chosen by the International Olympic Committee—ahead of Athens, Bangkok, Moscow and Turin—to host the first Youth Olympic Games. The games, scheduled to take place over 12 days in August 2010, will bring together more than 3,000 of the world's best young athletes aged between 14 and 18 from 202 countries to compete in 26 sporting events. Singapore offered 24 different venues for the event, with four to be built as temporary facilities, including one large cluster of 13 facilities in the Marina-Kallang area. The Youth Olympic Village will be located at a new multi-million-dollar student residential complex at the National University of Singapore, slated for completion months before the event.

The authorities announced that just over S$100 million will be spent on the event, from educational and cultural programmes to the development of services and transport.

244

Singapore Youth Olympic Games Organising Committee

Singapore will host the first Youth Olympic Games in 2010.

Singapore erupted in celebration after winning the right to host the inaugural Youth Olympics Games in 2010, with Prime Minister Lee Hsien Loong calling it a new era for Southeast Asian sport.

INTEGRATED RESORTS

The government loosened the apron strings a bit more in 2005 when it announced in April that the country would develop two resort-casino projects, known locally as integrated resorts. The decision came despite strong opposition expressed from citizens who feared an increase in gambling addiction and other problems commonly associated with legalized gambling.

Families Against the Casino Threat in Singapore, a group formed to oppose the project, collected more than 29,000 signatures on a petition against the integrated complexes. "Maybe a casino will provide jobs for about 4,000 people, but there will be more than that number of broken families," said Arthur Tan, a founder of the group.

246

AP Photos

Three nearly completed hotel towers (left) dominate the construction site for the Marina Bay Sands integrated resort, 2009.

This decision represented a complete turnabout from a blanket ban on casinos that had been in place since independence in 1965. At that time, Prime Minister Lee Kuan Yew had identified the fight against corruption and vice as a major priority, and the ban on casino gambling was a consequence of this. However, Singapore's priorities had changed with its radically different circumstances, and Lee Hsien Loong, who took over from Goh Chok Tong as prime minister in August 2004, identified a different set of challenges.

"We cannot stand still. The whole region is on the move. If we do not change, where will we be in 20 years' time? Losing our appeal to tourists is the lesser problem. But if we become a backwater, just one of many ordinary cities in Asia, instead of being a cosmopolitan hub of the region, then many good jobs will be lost and all Singaporeans will suffer. We cannot afford that," Lee Hsien Loong told Parliament, explaining the decision to allow the development of casinos.

The Marina Bay Sands includes a Waterfront Promenade that will be integrated with a grand, multi-level retail arcade combining civic space, shopping, indoor and outdoor areas with city skyline views and abundant greenery. At a cost of S$4.9 billion, Marina Bay Sands is scheduled to open in 2010 with three 50-storey hotel towers containing 1,000 rooms each and a two-acre Sky Garden bridging the towers. The plan for the complex also features outdoor amenities such as jogging paths, swimming pools, spas, and gardens, an arts and sciences museum on the promontory, an integrated waterside promenade and shopping arcade, a state-of-the art convention centre, two 2,000-seat theatres, a 4,000-car garage, and a casino.

The other complex, the S$5.2 billion Resorts World at Sentosa, also scheduled to open in 2010, is designed for family entertainment. Its collection of resorts within a resort will include the Universal Studios Singapore Theme Park, the Quest Marine Life Park, the Aquarius Water Park, and the Maritime Xperiential Museum, among others. The project envisages gourmet dining courtesy of world famous chefs and a state-of-the art spa centre. Resorts World will also have meeting and

247

Artist's rendering of Genting International's second casino and entertainment resort on Sentosa Island.

"What we were created to do we are now able to do again. It is almost like a return to the past."

– George Yeo, minister of foreign affairs, 2004

incentive facilities for up to 12,000 delegates in three meeting venues and seven indoor incentive venues. The project features six hotels.

The two integrated resorts are expected to attract investment of $5 billion and create some 35,000 jobs, including 10,000 positions within the integrated resorts themselves.

As Singapore approached the 200th anniversary of Raffle's landing on a swampy island at the southern tip of continental Asia, it's hard not to be impressed by the city's progress, particularly in the decades following its independence. With a heavy hand and a clear understanding of his situation, Lee Kuan Yew created a city-state that is hailed as free from corruption, healthy and safe, and a bastion for modern business. His successors have added to his achievements, moving with the times to maintain economic growth and social stability.

Critics—mostly from outside Singapore—suggest such success came at too high a price. They decry the lack of any real political opposition, censorship, and philosophy that puts national stability above personal freedoms. As Singapore moves forward, its leaders acknowledge that the times have changed, and policies that Lee Kuan Yew used to create a modern country may have to be revisited. The lifting of the ban on casinos is one illustration of this shift.

"City-states don't survive that long," said Mahbubani, the former UN ambassador. "They have flashes of brilliance for 50 years, 100 years, then they go. The eternal challenge for Singapore is how do we ensure that what we've had for these past 40 years is not just a brilliant flash that just goes away."

INDEX

251